Ruth: An Expositional Commentary

by
Cyril J. Barber

MOODY PRESS

CHICAGO

© 1983 by
THE MOODY BIBLE INSTITUTE
OF CHICAGO

All Scripture quotations, except where noted otherwise, are the author's
translation.

Library of Congress Cataloging in Publication Data

Barber, Cyril J.
  Ruth, an expositional commentary.

  Includes bibliographical references.
  1. Bible. O.T. Ruth—Commentaries. I. Title.
BS1315.3.B37 1983   222'.3507   83-7986
ISBN 0-8024-0184-8
                    1 2 3 4 5 6 7 Printing/EB/Year 87 86 85 84 83

Printed in the United States of America

*For my dear friend and pastor,
Dr. Charles R. Swindoll,
whose ministry to me through
the years has been a constant
source of encouragement and
blessing*

ACKNOWLEDGMENTS

The following publishers have graciously given permission for copyrighted material used in this book:

Doubleday and Company for permission to quote from E. F. Campbell's *Ruth* (Anchor Bible).

Harper's for the quote from the January 1976 issue of the magazine.

Harper and Row for the quote from O. Eissfeldt's *The Old Testament: An Introduction*.

Johns Hopkins University Press for permission to quote from W. F. Albright's *Archaeology and the Religion of Israel*; and J. M. Sasson's *Ruth, a New Translation with a Philological Commentary and a Formalist-Folklorist Interpretation*.

Keter Publishing House, Jerusalem, for the quote from M. Weinfeld's article on "Ruth" in the *Encyclopedia Judaica*.

Mack Publishing Company for permission to quote from D. A. Leggett's *Levirate and Goel Institutions in the Old Testament*.

Multnomah Press for the quote from Charles Swindoll's *Make Up Your Mind*.

Tyndale Press, London, for the quote from Leon Morris, *Ruth* (Tyndale Old Testament Commentaries).

ABBREVIATIONS

AJSL	*American Journal of Semitic Languages and Literatures*
ANET	*Ancient Near Eastern Texts,* edited by J. B. Pritchard. Princeton, N.J.: Princeton U., 1969.
Archer	*Survey of Old Testament Introduction,* by G. L. Archer. Chicago: Moody, 1974.
BA	*Biblical Archaeologist*
BASOR	*Bulletin of the American Society for Oriental Research*
BDB	*Hebrew-English Lexicon of the Old Testament,* edited by F. Brown, S. R. Driver, and C. A. Briggs. Oxford: Clarendon, 1953.
Bewer	*Literature of the Old Testament,* by J. A. Bewer. New York: Columbia U., 1933.
BJRL	*Bulletin of the John Rylands Library*
BT	*Bible Translator*
Campbell	*Ruth, a New Translation with Introduction, Notes, and Commentary,* by E. F. Campbell, Jr. *The Anchor Bible.* Garden City, N.Y.: Doubleday, 1975.
Cassell	*Joshua, Judges and Ruth,* by P. Cassell (in J. P. Lange's *Commentary on the Holy Scriptures*). Grand Rapids: Zondervan, n.d.
CBQ	*Catholic Biblical Quarterly*
Cox	*The Book of Ruth,* by S. Cox. London: Religious Tract Society, 1922.
de Vaux	*Ancient Israel,* by R. de Vaux. Translated by J. McHugh. New York: McGraw-Hill, 1961.
Driver	*Introduction to the Literature of the Old Testament,* by S. R. Driver. Edinburgh: T. & T. Clark, 1913.

EQ	*Evangelical Quarterly*
ET	*Expository Times*
Fuerst	"Ruth," *Cambridge Bible Commentary,* by W. J. Fuerst. New York: Cambridge U., 1975.
Fuller	*A Comment on Ruth,* by T. Fuller. Minneapolis: Klock and Klock, 1983.
Gerleman	*Ruth Das Hoheleid,* by G. Gerleman. Biblischer Kommentar Altes Testament. Neukirchen Kreis Moers: Buchhandlung des Erziehungsvereins, 1965.
Gray	*Joshua, Judges, Ruth,* by J. Gray. New Century Bible. Grand Rapids: Eerdmans, 1967.
Harrison	*Introduction to the Old Testament,* by R. K. Harrison. Grand Rapids: Eerdmans, 1969.
HDB	*Dictionary of the Bible,* edited by J. Hastings. Edinburgh: T. & T. Clark, 1902.
Hertzberg	*Die Bücher Josua, Richter, Ruth,* by H. W. Hertzberg. *Das Alte Testament Deutsch.* Göttingen: Vandenhoeck and Ruprecht, 1959.
HTR	*Harvard Theological Review*
IBD	*Illustrated Bible Dictionary,* edited by J. D. Douglas. Wheaton, Ill.: Tyndale House, 1980.
JAOS	*Journal of the American Oriental Society*
JBL	*Journal of Biblical Literature*
JBR	*Journal of Bible and Religion*
JNES	*Journal of Near Eastern Studies*
Joüon, *Grammaire*	*Grammaire de l'hebreu biblique,* by P. Joüon. Rome: Pontifical Biblical Institute, 1923.
Joüon, *Ruth*	*Ruth, Commentaire Philologique et Exegetique,* by P. Joüon. Rome: Pontifical Biblical Institute, 1953.
JRAS	*Journal of the Royal Asiatic Society*
JTS	*Journal of Theological Studies*
KD	*Biblical Commentary on the Old Testament,* 10 vols., by C. F. Keil and F. J. Delitzsch. Grand Rapids: Eerdmans, n.d.
Kennedy	*The Book of Ruth,* by A. R. S. Kennedy. New York: Macmillan, 1928.
Leggett	*The Levirate and Goel Institutions in the Old Testament, with Special Reference to the Book of Ruth,* by D. A. Leggett. Cherry Hill, N.J.: Mack Publishing, 1974.

Morison	*Ruth,* by J. Morison. The Pulpit Commentary. Grand Rapids: Eerdmans, 1963.
Morris	*Ruth,* by L. L. Morris. Tyndale Old Testament Commentaries. Downer's Grove, Ill.: Inter-Varsity Press, 1968.
Myers	*The Linguistic and Literary Form of the Book of Ruth,* by J. M. Myers. Leiden: E. J. Brill, 1955.
PEQ	*Palestinian Exploration Quarterly*
Robinson	*Biblical Researches in Palestine,* by E. Robinson. London: John Murray, 1856.
Rudolph.	*Das Buch Ruth, Das Hohe Lied, Die Klagelieder,* by W. Rudolph. Kommentar zum Alten Testament. Gütersloh: J. C. Mohr, 1962.
Sasson	*Ruth, a New Translation with a Philological Commentary and a Formalist-Folklorist Interpretation,* by J. M. Sasson. Baltimore: Johns Hopkins U., 1979.
Taylor	*Ruth the Gleaner,* by W. M. Taylor. Grand Rapids: Baker, 1961.
TDOT	*Theological Dictionary of the Old Testament,* edited by G. J. Botterweck and H. Ringgren. Grand Rapids: Eerdmans, 1974.
TWOT	*Theological Wordbook of the Old Testament,* edited by R. F. Harris, G. L. Archer, and B. K. Waltke. Chicago: Moody, 1980.
VT	*Vetus Testamentum*
Watson	*The Book of Ruth,* by R. A. Watson. The Expositor's Bible. New York: A. C. Armstrong, 1898.
Wright	*The Book of Ruth in Hebrew,* by C. H. H. Wright. Leipzig: Rudolph Hartmann, 1864.
ZPEB	*Zondervan Pictorial Encyclopedia of the Bible,* edited by M. C. Tenney. Grand Rapids: Zondervan, 1975.

CONTENTS

FOREWORD

At the foot of the gray ridge on which the city of Bethlehem was built lie the "shepherds' fields," where flocks used in the sacrifices at Jerusalem were pastured by Temple shepherds. There also stood the shepherds' watchtower—the tower of the flock, or *Middol Eder*—where, according to Micah, dominion would come to the daughter of Zion (Mic. 4:8). Bethlehem was certainly the birthplace of David (1 Sam. 16), but Micah anticipated that night when the tower of the flock would be bathed in celestial light and surrounded by angelic hosts (Luke 2:9), for it was in Bethlehem that the Supreme Ruler of Israel would be born (Mic. 5:2).

One can picture the excited shepherds leaving their flocks and making their way up the terraced hill to the summit, guided only by the light of the lamp swung from the rope across the entrance to the local inn, to find a newborn babe in the inn's filthy courtyard. The inn has long since disappeared, but there is little doubt that the Church of the Nativity stands today upon the authentic site. The evidence of the centuries is too strong to dispute.

But centuries earlier those fields below were covered with grain and were the possession of a middle-aged farmer of Bethlehem. It was in those fields that Ruth the Moabitess gleaned, and it was there and on that hillside that the scenes of the most delightful idyll of the book of Ruth occurred. Before the inn was built on the hill's summit the house of the wealthy Boaz stood there, and before the courtyard was occupied by cattle and donkeys the open space was a threshing floor.

It would be difficult to find a city gate in Bethlehem today, but the old city of Jerusalem provides the picture. It was in that open space around the inside of the gate that the commercial bargains were struck—with all the haggling and argument that still go on. Here also the old men of the city would gather to sit upon the ground or upon the stones and discuss the problems of the day. It was they whose wisdom was sought by those with difficulties; it was to them that cases were brought for discussion and

11

decision, and the passing crowds would listen to their lengthy arguments and judgments. Few would question the wisdom of the elders or their conclusions.

It is still possible to imagine the self-possessed Boaz standing among them and accosting his relative in order that his problem might be solved.

How real it all seems, yet how remote from the present day! Or is it? Cyril Barber has deftly and capably demonstrated the relevance of Ruth's story to the present day. Not only has he given us an extremely satisfying exposition of the Old Testament book, but he has deduced from it many lessons that are pertinent to us in our late twentieth-century circumstances. The references in the appendix indicate the extent of his research and the breadth of his reading, and we are consequently his debtors. Here is a book that deserves to be read—and then re-read. I wholeheartedly commend it.

                                                          Frederick A. Tatford

PREFACE

In his fine treatment of the book of Ruth, the famous Scottish preacher William M. Taylor related an incident from the life of Benjamin Franklin.

It is said that Dr. Franklin was once in the company of several ladies of the English nobility, when the conversation turned upon pastoral poetry. The ladies took a considerable part in the discussion, and after hearing their criticisms on various authors, the doctor offered to read the translation of a pastoral for their amusement. He read, with a few verbal alterations, the Book of Ruth. They were enraptured, pronounced it the finest they had ever heard from any language, and insisted upon knowing whose it was. Imagine their confusion when he told them that he had read it from the Bible.

The story of the book of Ruth may be better known today, but its message still appears wrapped in obscurity. In fact, very few expositions of Ruth have been published in English in the last one hundred years, and there are less than a handful that are worthy of a reader's time and attention.

The neglect of the teaching of Ruth was brought home to me quite forcefully several years ago when the pastor of a suburban church near our home became ill. I was asked to fill the pulpit during his absence. Because I did not know how many Sundays would be involved, I chose a portion from Ruth for each Sunday morning's exposition.

In seeking for useful exegetical and expository material I found that the only English work to have been published in recent years had been written by the renowned Australian Bible scholar Leon Morris (1968). Then, in the same year that I delivered the messages on Ruth (1975), Edward F. Campbell, Jr., had his commentary published in the Anchor Bible.

Two other studies have also appeared: Donald A. Leggett's *The Levirate and Goel Institutions in the Old Testament* (1974), and Jack M. Sasson's *Ruth, a New Translation with a Philological Commentary and a Formalist-Folklorist Interpretation* (1979). Both of these works were prepared as dissertations.

I believe it is important for an expositor to be familiar with matters of criticism and interpretation. However, I also believe the Scriptures to be the inspired and inerrant Word of God to man. Many modern, esoteric approaches to the text detract from the theme of a book and leave the needy searcher bereft of spiritual nourishment, counsel, and direction. It has therefore been my desire, after careful study, to follow the biblical text as closely as possible and allow its teachings to emerge unfettered by critical assumptions.

These studies were originally given as messages on the book of Ruth and then published in two magazines, one domestic and the other foreign. Then I reworked the material entirely for a series of weekly Bible studies given to the library staff of the International Christian Graduate University, San Bernardino, California, where I happened to be serving as a consultant. Those readings were based upon the Masoretic text, and they are reproduced here in the same informal manner in which they were delivered.

Between the delivery of the earlier expository messages and the informal Bible studies with the library staff of the university, I kept returning to the theme of Ruth—which I believe reveals the grace of God in the Old Testament. Now that my investigation into the teaching of this important portion of God's revelation is drawing to a close, I trust that what follows will be read with profit by all who study this brief but crucial section of God's Word.

In publishing these studies, no claim is made for my erudition! I have endeavored to do what all preachers and teachers do. I have researched each passage as thoroughly as my time and the reference works at my disposal would allow. Certain books and journal articles were not available to me. I am sure that had I had access to those materials the content of this slender volume would have been much improved.

Although I freely acknowledge the benefit derived from reflecting on what others have written, no attempt has been made to synthesize their exemplary studies and serve them up as if they were my own. I regard their contributions as unique, and the worst disservice that could be done some of the older writers would be to sully their treatment with a superficial modern restatement. As I prepared these studies I reflected on the central teaching of each passage and then tried to provide the listener with something that I hoped would be both timely and relevant.

Because it is important for each one of us in *studying* the Bible to follow the text of Scripture as closely as possible, I have throughout supplied my own translation. This may at first seem to be a pedantic exercise; however, because there are many excellent paraphrases and translations of the Bible on the market—each aiming at fluidity of style and contemporaneity of expression—I may perhaps be forgiven the literalness of my translation. But there is another reason why I have included my own rendering of the Hebrew text. Numerous peculiarities are to be found in the original that may not come out in a translation. These are often of great importance in understanding what God has revealed, and the only way to draw attention to these nuances and idiosyncrasies in the original writer's style is through a literal translation.

A further word of explanation needs to be made about what follows. Because these studies of the book of Ruth were delivered weekly, a certain amount of repetition was inevitable. I trust that my readers will pardon this seeming redundancy. It is difficult to avoid reiteration of certain truths when key thoughts and phrases continuously are encountered in the biblical text.

I would like to thank sincerely those whose helpfulness and encouragement have meant a great deal to me. First, my dear wife, Aldyth, whose unfailing support means so much to me; second, my good friend Mr. John Gamble of Emerald Island Books, Belfast, Northern Ireland, who secured for me hard-to-find copies of Thomas Fuller's *A Comment on Ruth* and Edward Robinson's *Biblical Researches*—works that I was able to put to good use in this study; third, to Mr. Gerald L. Gooden, librarian, Biola University, who graciously made available to me the resources of his institution; fourth, to my dear friends Mrs. Les (Ellen) Beery, Mrs. Michael (Marilyn) Moore, and Mrs. Dan (Alberta) Smith, who typed and retyped the manuscript; and finally to Dr. Frederick A. Tatford, renowned British Bible teacher and fellow countryman, for so graciously reading this work and supplying the Foreword.

Introduction

F. F. Bruce, the renowned British Bible scholar, has appropriately observed that "the Bible was never intended to be a book for scholars and specialists only. From the very beginning it was intended to be everybody's book, and that is what it continues to be."

In the books that make up the Old and New Testaments, God has seen fit to disclose Himself to us and impart truths important for us to learn. His revelation has been both purposeful and progressive. Each book of the Bible, therefore, has a distinct theme, and each enlarges our understanding of His will for us (Heb. 1:1-2).

The Old Testament has long been neglected. The emphasis in our modern culture has been upon the writings of the New Testament, for in them we read of Christ and the salvation He came to bring. We cut ourselves off from a rich storehouse of knowledge, however, if we lose sight of the teachings contained in the Old Testament. As Augustine observed, *"The New* [Testament] *is in the Old concealed; the Old is in the New revealed."*

One of the Old Testament books that we generally have some knowledge of is the book of Ruth. But as we mentally rehearse the facts, can we say with equal certainty that we understand why God included it in the Bible? What are we to learn from this brief story? Paul wrote that "these things happened [to those living in Old Testament times] as examples for us . . . and they were written for our instruction" (1 Cor. 10:6, 11). What timeless truths from Ruth impress you and me today with their importance and relevance? If the only value of such reflection is in the appreciation of interpersonal relationships of two women, then we have benefited from only a superficial grasp of the contents.

HAND OF THE POTTER

The book of Ruth has been described as a "veritable masterpiece of the storyteller's art."[1] It is complete with symmetry of form, characteriza-

17

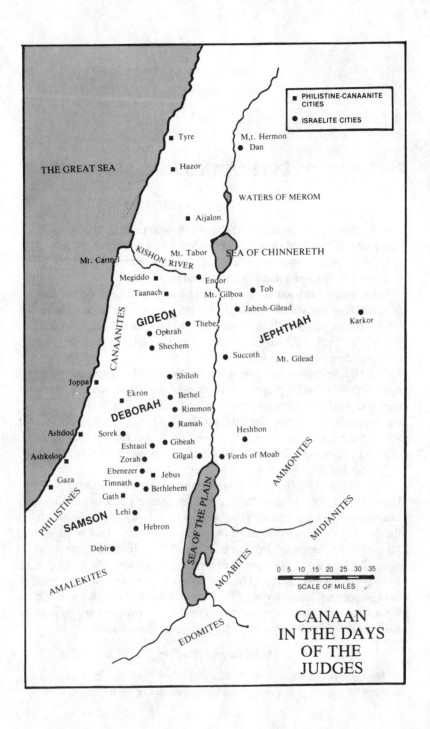

THE GREAT SEA

■ Tyre

● M,t. Hermon
● Dan

● Hazor

WATERS OF MEROM

■ Aijalon

KISHON RIVER

Mt. Carmel

Mt. Tabor

SEA OF CHINNERETH

Megiddo ■

● Endor

Taanach ■

Mt. Gilboa ● Tob

CANAANITES

Jabesh-Gilead

● Karkor

GIDEON

● Thebez

JEPHTHAH

● Ophrah

● Shechem

● Succoth

Mt. Gilead

● Shiloh

Joppa ■

Ekron ■ ● Bethel

DEBORAH

● Rimmon

● Ramah

Ashdod ■

Sorek ●

Heshbon ●

AMMONITES

Ashkelon ■

Eshtaol ● Gibeah

Zorah ● Gilgal ● ● Fords of Moab

Gaza ■

Ebenezer ● Jebus

Timnath ● ● Bethlehem

MIDIANITES

Gath ■

SAMSON

Lehi ●

PHILISTINES

● Hebron

SEA OF THE PLAIN

Debir ●

0 5 10 15 20 25 30 35

AMALEKITES

MOABITES

SCALE OF MILES

EDOMITES

CANAAN
IN THE DAYS
OF THE
JUDGES

■	PHILISTINE-CANAANITE CITIES
●	ISRAELITE CITIES

tion, human emotion, restraint, dignity, and a pleasing repetitive style that fits well the mannerisms of those we read about. The story moves easily from the small hamlet of Bethlehem across the River Jordan to Moab, and then back to Bethlehem. But more than geography is involved. The book is about people, their problems and personal concerns. It is also about God. The narrative is developed primarily through conversations clustered around six scenes. Each scene reflects a complicated network of human emotion.[2]

Initially, therefore, the book may be outlined as follows:

Introduction, 1:1-5
1. In Moab, 1:6-18
2. In Bethlehem, 1:19-22
3. In the Harvest Fields, 2:1-23
4. On the Threshing Floor, 3:1-18
5. Sitting in the Gate, 4:1-12
6. In the Home of Boaz, 4:13-17
   Epilogue, 4:18-22

DRAMATIS PERSONAE

Like the characters in one of Shakespeare's plays, each person in the book of Ruth has an important role. Those people are:

Elimelech ("My God is King"), husband of Naomi
Naomi ("Pleasant, delightful, lovely"), wife of Elimelech
Mahlon ("Weakness" or "Sickness"?), son of Elimelech and Naomi and husband of Ruth
Chilion ("Pining" or "Consumption"?), son of Elimelech and Naomi and husband of Orpah
Ruth ("Friend"?), wife of Mahlon
Orpah ("Firmness"?), wife of Chilion
Boaz ("in Him is strength"), a relative of Elimelech
People of Bethlehem
Elders of the city
A foreman in the field
Workers in the harvest field
An unnamed kinsman

HISTORICAL BACKDROP

MIGRATION OF THE FAMILY

The story is set in the time when the judges "judged" (governed or ruled) the tribes of Israel.[3] It tells of a famine that threatened the livelihood of Elimelech and his family. A decision, therefore, was reached, and in order to save their temporal possessions they set out for Moab (1:1-2). The initial stay in Moab soon took on the nature of settled residency. Furthermore, Elimelech died (1:3), leaving Naomi a widow.

Mahlon and Chilion married Moabite women, Ruth and Orpah, and resided in the land for about ten years. Each couple, however, remained childless. When Mahlon and Chilion also died, the three widows were left desolate and destitute (1:4-5).

Naomi determined to return to Judah, for she could no longer live and maintain herself respectably in a foreign land. Her sorrowing daughters-in-law started to accompany her. Naomi, however, sensed the impracticality of their decision and in an impassioned and noble statement insisted that each return to her mother's home (1:8-13). Orpah relented, but Ruth refused to heed Naomi's remonstrance (1:14). In words of exquisite beauty she says:

> Insist not on me forsaking thee,
> To return from following after thee:
> For whither thou goest, I will go;
> And wheresoever thou lodgest, I will lodge:
> Thy people [will be] my people,
> And thy God [will be] my God;
> Wheresoever thou diest, I will die,
> And there will I be buried.
> So may *Yahweh* do to me,
> And still more,
> If aught but death part thee and me.
>
> 1:16-17

So Ruth accompanied Naomi to Bethlehem. The two widows, the one old and beyond the age of bearing children and the other young and in the prime of life, faced a bleak future. But their hearts had been knit together in mutual affection, and as we shall see, each would look out for the other.

As Naomi and Ruth entered, travel-worn and weary, the small village of Bethlehem, the women of the town came out to see them. The women faintly recognized Naomi after an absence of ten years and exclaimed, "Is this Naomi?" The recollection of the meaning of her name caused Naomi to say with pain and sadness of heart, "Do not call me Naomi [meaning "pleasantness"] but call me Mara [meaning "bitterness"] for *Shaddai* ["the Almighty"] has dealt very bitterly with me" (1:18-21).

God in His grace, however, had brought Naomi and Ruth back to Judah at the beginning of the barley harvest. They would not be destitute (1:22).

OLD TESTAMENT BIBLE CHRONOLOGY

—H. G. Hendricks

PROVISION FOR THE FAMILY

With the gnawing reality of hunger, Ruth asked Naomi for permission to go to the fields and glean what the reapers had left behind. In the providence of God, Ruth "happened" to choose a section of the field belonging to Boaz. She knew nothing of his relationship to her late father-in-law and asked the overseer only for permission to glean in the field (2:1-3).

Shortly before midday Boaz came from the city and greeted the reapers cordially. Then he noticed the stranger and inquired, "Whose young woman is this?" The overseer informed him, and Boaz instructed the workers to treat her with courtesy and respect. He also spoke to Ruth and encouraged her. Later, at the noon meal, he invited her to join him (2:4-16).

Ruth labored all day and at sunset threshed the grain from the husks. She then took what she had gleaned, together with some of her leftovers from lunch, and retured to Naomi. Naomi's hunger was such that she did not inquire of Ruth how matters went until after she had eaten. When she heard that it was in Boaz's field that Ruth had gleaned, she said, "This man is our relative, [in fact] he is one of our closest relatives" (2:17-23).

Ruth continued to glean in the fields of Boaz until the end of the wheat harvest. When the winnowing of the grain began, Naomi suggested to Ruth that she ask Boaz to marry her. The provision for such a union had been established in antiquity (Gen. 38) and was a part of the settled tradition of God's ancient people Israel (Deut. 25:5-10).

Ruth acceded to Naomi's plan (3:1-5). She went down to the threshing floor and took note of the place where Boaz was sleeping. When all was quiet and the men were evidently asleep, Ruth lay down at his feet. During the night, as Boaz moved, he sensed that somebody was with him. Ruth identified herself and requested that Boaz fulfill the obligations of a kinsman by marrying her (3:6-9).

Boaz was moved by Ruth's loyalty to the traditions of his people and her desire to care for Naomi by marrying within the family, and he praised her. He also assured her that he would do as she had requested, but informed her that there was a relative nearer of kin to Elimelech than he, and that this relative had the right of first refusal (3:10-12)!

Ruth remained on the threshing floor with Boaz until the darkness began to fade with the approaching dawn. Boaz then sent her back to Naomi with six measures of barley as a token of his intention to fulfill his word (3:13-18).

REDEMPTION OF THE FAMILY

Early the next morning Boaz took his place at the gate of the city. When

the man who was nearer of kin to Elimelech than he passed by, Boaz
called to him. The words *peloni almoni* ("Turn aside, friend") informed
the kinsman that Boaz had a legal matter to transact with him.

Boaz then impaneled ten of the most trustworthy elders of the city and
advised Naomi's kinsman that Elimelech's widow, on account of her
poverty, was compelled to sell the piece of land that formerly belonged to
her husband. Boaz then began to press home his point by recommending
that this relative buy the land from Naomi. He assured him, however, that
should he not wish to do so, then he (Boaz) would perform the duty of
kinsman. Boaz's relative ignored the offer and expressed his willingness
to buy the land (4:2-4).

But Boaz was not finished. He informed his unnamed relative: "On the
day you buy the field from the hand of Naomi, you must also acquire Ruth
the Moabitess, the widow of the deceased, in order to raise up the name of
the deceased on his inheritance (4:5)." The anonymous kinsman was
unwilling to take Ruth and Naomi into his home and declined to accept
the terms. He then took off his shoe and gave it to Boaz, symbolically
transferring to him the right to plant his foot (i.e., take possession) of all
that was formerly his (4:1-8).

From that point on the story hastens toward its conclusion. In the
presence of those gathered to witness the transaction, Boaz stated that he
would not only buy Naomi's land, but also take Ruth to be his wife
(4:9-12). The elders of the city and the people pronounced a benediction
upon Boaz:

> May [*Yahweh*] make the woman who is coming into your home like Rachel and
> Leah, both of whom built the house of Israel; and may you achieve wealth in
> Ephrathah and become famous in Bethlehem. Moreover, may your house be
> like the house of Perez whom Tamar bore to Judah, through the offspring which
> the Lord shall give you by this young woman. [4:11-12]

The Lord enabled Ruth to conceive and she bore a son, who was called
Obed (meaning "servant").

The story closes by bringing to the attention of the reader two
important facts: (1) The Lord fully compensated Naomi for the loss of her
husband and sons (4:15-17); and (2) unknown to her, Ruth became the
great grandmother of King David (4:18-22), and now stands in the
ancestral line of the Lord Jesus Christ (Matthew 1:5).

With this brief summary before us we can now consider the authorship
and date of the book, its place in the canon, and the purpose or theme of
this brief work. In order to obviate extensive discussion of some points—
discussion made necessary by much negative biblical criticism—

technical details and other documentation will be confined to footnotes included in the Appendix.

AUTHORSHIP AND DATE OF RUTH

AUTHORSHIP

The book of Ruth was anonymously written. According to Jewish tradition,[4] Samuel wrote it as well as Judges. Modern Bible scholars are inclined to reject this idea, for Ruth 4:17-22 traces the descendants from the union of Boaz and Ruth through Obed and Jesse to David, and Samuel died before David ascended the throne (1 Sam. 25:1).

Before we dismiss Samuel's involvement too quickly, let us recall that the events of Ruth are set in the time of the judges (Ruth 1:1), and that Samuel was both a prophet and a judge. The book of Judges closes with an "appendix" (Judg. 17-21) in which we are given a glimpse of the spiritual and moral conditions of that era. Chapters 17 and 18 describe Israel's spiritual apostasy and show how rife was her infidelity. Chapters 19 through 21 describe the nadir of the people's moral degradation, recording their unbridled desire for revenge. Both stories concern the village of "Bethlehem in Judah" (Judges 17:7-9; 19:2, 18), and much of the contents of Ruth is enacted in this city. It should not surprise us, therefore, if the author of Judges also wrote the book of Ruth.

Others object to Samuel's possible authorship on the grounds that the genealogy at the end of the book is "intended to show how the ancestors of the great king walked uprightly before God and man in piety of life."[5] They also find evidence, and rightfully so, of the composition of the book *after* the events it describes (cf. 1:1; 4:7 as well as 4:18-22). How much later still needs to be determined.

In the interest of an objective investigation and evaluation of the facts, let it be remembered that David is *not* spoken of as being king in 4:22; Samuel did anoint him to be king in the place of Saul even though it was more than ten years before he ascended the throne (1 Sam. 16:12-14).

Furthermore, the removal of the shoe in 4:7 is supposedly a reference to a long unused custom. It could easily refer to Deuteronomy 25:9-10— a work penned by Moses before the Israelites entered the promised land (1400 B.C.)[6]—which, according to C. F. Keil, preceded the events of our story by 150 to 180 years.

Further evidence that must be weighed comes from 1 and 2 Samuel. They contain no particulars respecting the ancestry of David, even though a genealogy was frequently given for Hebrew kings. What could better explain the omission of David's genealogy in 1 Samuel than the fact that such data had already been given in the book of Ruth?

But in conclusion it must be admitted that internal evidence gives no indication of authorship.[7] It does, however, point to a date of composition much earlier than generally allowed by Bible scholars.

DATE

The Old Testament scholar C. F. Keil assigned the book of Ruth to the period of the early monarchy. He is followed in that by R. K. Harrison and E. J. Young.[8] Other writers prefer a date between David's reign and the Babylonian captivity (971-605 B.C.). Various possibilities are suggested; the "Solomonic enlightenment," the reign of Hezekiah, or a time immediately following the death of Athaliah.[9] A few writers believe the book was written during the exilic period (605-536 B.C.);[10] the majority, however, favor a postexilic date (538-400 B.C.).[11] C. Cornill provides a succinct summary of the arguments in favor of a late date.

> Other grounds exist which favour a later time as the time of its composition. The time-indication in the days when the judges judged (i. 1) presupposes the rigidly fixed chronological system of the Deuteronomic Exile History of Israel. The language of the book is strongly tinged with Aramaisms, and has many peculiarities which point with convincing and cogent force to the post-exilic period; while, on the other hand, the recital itself is mainly composed of reminiscences of older historical works, especially J [the "Yahwistic" or "Jehovistic" writer]. Quite a striking and convincing example is to be seen in Ruth iv. 7 compared with Deut. xxv. 9; here a custom which was current in the times of Deuteronomy is expressly explained as if it were an antiquarian curiosity. The conclusion (iv. 18-22), which displays the schematic arrangement of the genealogies of P [the "Priestly" writer] had better be left out of account, because it may have been added later as the completion of vs. 12.[12]

J. Myers, however, lists a series of *archaic* Hebrew forms in Ruth,[13] which are difficult to reconcile with a late date of composition.

G. Gerleman likewise takes issue with those who wish to see several stages in the transmission of the book or who, for slender reasons, persist in ignoring the historical evidence for an earlier date. He states:

> One could no longer talk about David and his lineage in the exilic period in such an unbiased fashion as it happens in the story of Ruth. . . . It must have been a very definite and compelling reason which caused the writer of Ruth to tell his story. . . . The notice, which connects David with Boaz and Ruth, is no secondary addition to an old story. On the contrary, this seemingly casual notice is to be viewed as an original kernel for which reason the Ruth story was written.[14]

Although I disagree with Gerleman's understanding of the purpose of the book of Ruth, I agree with his statement advocating the unity of the original composition and his argument from Israel's history. If the book of Ruth had *not* been based on a true and contemporary account of actual events, it would *never* have been invented in later days. The hatred of Moab, which was felt by the people of Israel and expressed by the prophets (Amos 2:1-3; Jer. 48; Ezek. 25:8-11), would never have allowed Israel's greatest king to be thought of as descending from a Moabite woman.

The problem associated with the "antiquarian" interest (particularly as seen in 4:1-12) really surrounds the dating of the book of Deuteronomy. If this work is assigned to Moses and dated shortly before 1400 B.C., then sufficient time would have elapsed for the teachings of Moses to become obscured and for the Word of the Lord to be forgotten. It must be remembered that with a central sanctuary in which the Ark of the Covenant was kept (and with it the only extant copy of God's Word), the people were totally dependent upon the ministry of the priests and Levites for instruction. As the religious leaders became apostate (after the time of Joshua and the elders who outlived him), judges had to be raised up to bring the people back to the ways of the Lord. If the events of the book of Ruth are assigned to the early period of Gideon's life (c. 1191-1151 B.C.),[15] then fully two centuries elapsed following the penning of Deuteronomy. That allows ample time for certain customs to fall into disuse!

Second, growing out of the assigning of documentary sources (J, E, D, and P) to many of the books of the Old Testament, it is not surprising that Bible critics see the book of Ruth as supposedly containing evidence of Yahwistic (J) and Priestly (P) influence. Of this negative trend in biblical criticism Samuel M. Zwemer observed, "One reads with astonishment how the simple Scripture narrative was made both incredible and unintelligible in their [i.e., the redactor's, editor's, or reviser's] hands. Their method was by pedantic analysis, illogical presumptions and anti-supernatural bias to refuse any quarter to the inspired writers."[16]

Even Winston Churchill, as learned a literary genius as ever lived, denounced this approach to the study of Scripture. He remarked:

> We reject with scorn all these learned and labored myths. . . . We believe that the most scientific view, the most up-to-date and rationalistic conception, will find its fullest satisfaction in taking the Bible literally. . . . We may be sure that all things happened just as they are set out according to Holy Writ. The impressions these people received were faithfully recorded and have been transmitted across the centuries with far more accuracy than many of the telegraphed accounts of goings-on today. In the words of a forgotten work of Mr. Gladstone, we rest with assurance upon "The impregnable rock of Holy Scripture." Let the learned men of science and learning expand their

knowledge . . . and prove with their research every detail of the records which
have been preserved for us from those dim ages. All they will do is to fortify the
grand simplicity and essential accuracy of the recorded truths which have
lighted so far the pilgrimage of man.[17]

Other arguments in favor of a late date for the book of Ruth are (1) its
place in the third division of the Hebrew Bible (with the *Megilloth*), and
(2) the claim that the book was written to combat the supposed
"exclusivism" of Ezra and Nehemiah. These criticisms will be discussed
below under the canonicity of Ruth and the intention of God behind the
composition of the book.

For our purpose, after having duly consulted the writings of biblical
scholars, there seems to be no compelling reason for not assigning the
writing of this pastoral idyll to the period following David's anointing by
Samuel, or early in his reign in Hebron. Thus, we would date the events
of chapter 1 as possibly transpiring between 1198-1185 B.C. (during the
Midianite oppression that lasted from 1198-1191). The written record
could easily have been made between 1025-1005 B.C., if not by Samuel,
then perhaps by Nathan or someone attached to David's court.

The place of writing is unknown and would obviously be associated
with the author: Ramah, if Samuel wrote it; any one of the residences of
David, if composed during his "outlaw" years; or Hebron.

Having considered the difficulties surrounding the authorship and date
of the book of Ruth—difficulties made even more perplexing by the
many views held by Bible scholars—we now need to consider the
canonicity of Ruth and its place in the Hebrew Bible. As we do so, we will
discover how important this subject is and why it has led many writers to
assign Ruth a late date of composition.

THE QUESTION OF QUALITY

The word *canon* (from the Greek *kanōn*, meaning "rule"[18]) may have
been derived from the Hebrew *qänĕh,* "measuring rod." In the course of
time the term was used to designate the sum total of those books of the
Old Testament that were considered sacred by the Hebrews.

Shortly before the dawn of the Christian era the Jews began referring to
their sacred writings as those books that "defile the hands."[19] What this
Semiticism originally signified no one definitely knows. It is possible that
a passage of Scripture like Leviticus 16:24 contains a hint as to the
meaning of the expression. According to this portion of the law, on the
Day of Atonement the high priest washed not only when he put on the
garments of his office, *but also when he took them off.* Quite possibly,

therefore, the expression "to defile the hands," when used in connection with God's holy Word, signified that the hands that had touched the sacred writings must first be washed before touching anything else. If that were not done, then the ceremonial purity of the Scriptures might not be maintained.

DISPUTE OVER NUMBERS

The number of books composing the Hebrew canon is variously given as twenty-two and twenty-four. Josephus, a Jewish historian of the first century A.D., in handing down the tradition of his people said:

> For we have not an innumerable multitude of books among us, disagreeing from and contradicting one another [as the Greeks have], but only twenty-two, which contain the records of all the past times; which are justly believed to be divine; and of them, five belong to Moses, which contain the laws, and the traditions of the origin of mankind till his death . . . but as to the time from the death of Moses till the reign of Artaxerxes, king of Persia, who reigned after Xerxes, the prophets, who were after Moses, wrote down what was done in their time in thirteen books. The remaining four books contain hymns to God, and precepts for the conduct of human life. It is true that our history has been written since Artaxerxes, very particularly, but has not been esteemed of the like authority with the former by our forefathers.[20]

In Josephus's enumeration, Judges and Ruth were evidently counted as one book, as were Jeremiah and Lamentations.[21] The Talmud and the Midrash list twenty-four books. In those lists Ruth is separated from Judges and Lamentations from Jeremiah.

The inclusion of the book of Ruth in the canon of Scripture has never been seriously questioned. Its *position* in the canon, however, has been the subject of endless debate.

EARLY SUBDIVISION

Later on, the Old Testament Scriptures were grouped together as follows:[22]

The Books of the Old Testament

Law	Prophets		Writings
	Former	*Latter*	
Genesis—			Poetical
Deuteronomy	Joshua—	Isaiah—	Five Rolls
	2 Kings	Malachi	Historical

As early as the translation of the Hebrew Scriptures into Greek (c. 260 B.C.), the book of Ruth occupied a place between Judges and 1 Samuel.[23] This was verified by Melito of Sardis (died c. 190).[24] Further evidence for including Ruth with the writings of the Former Prophets comes from a very old Hebrew-Aramaic enumeration of the books of the Old Testament. Listed as MS. 54 of the library of the Greek patriarchate in Jerusalem, this manuscript may be the oldest listing of the canonical books available.[25] Its order (as far as it concerns our present study) is: Genesis, Exodus, Leviticus, Joshua, Deuteronomy, Numbers, Ruth, Job, and Judges. The important point to notice is that Ruth was included *with* the historical books of the Old Testament and *not* with the "Writings."

The biblical scholar Jerome (c. A.D. 340-420), who lived for many years in Antioch and spent the last thirty-five years of his life in Bethlehem, knew of the twenty-two book arrangement referred to by Josephus. Jerome was the first to refer to the *Kethûbîm* or "Writings"[26] as a distinct part of the canon. The gathering together of these Old Testament books into a distinct group is, therefore, of late origin.

But what significance does all of this have for the book of Ruth?

ORIGIN OF OUR *MYTH* CONCEPTIONS

Because the Jews (in about the fourth century A.D.) placed certain books together in a group for use at different festivals, modern scholars have assigned the writing of Ruth to a date much later than the biblical evidence warrants. Their reasoning runs something like this: "Ruth cannot have been written until *after* the 'canon of the prophets' had closed. Therefore an early date of composition is out of the question."[27] And with the assigning of a late date comes the distortion of the purpose or theme of the book.

In defense of this theory, and in an endeavor to preserve the authenticity of those books included in the Hebrew Bible, those who adhere to this view invariably claim that the issue of canonicity was not finally settled until the Council of Jamnia (A.D. 90).[28]

In response to that assertion, we may cite the book of Habakkuk (c. 615 B.C.) as an illustration of an *early* recognition that "God has spoken." In 1:5-11, the prophet was given a vision of Judah's pending destruction at the hands of the Chaldeans. In 2:2 he was told to inscribe the message of the Lord on tablets, so that the one who read it might take warning and flee the city.

If we are to apply artificial criteria of canonicity to this portion of God's Word, then the Word of the Lord through Habakkuk was not received by the Jews as authoritative until formally designated as "defiling the hands." That did not happen until much later when the "canon of the prophets" was closed. By that time it would have been too late for anyone to take warning (for Nebuchadnezzar took the city in 605 B.C.)!

On biblical grounds it seems preferable to conclude that the pious in Israel, upon either hearing or reading His Word, recognized instinctively that God had spoken. Scripture, therefore, was immediately recognized as normative by those who were God-fearing. It was not necessary for them to wait for some council to grant its approval before the books of the Old Testament could be regarded as authoritative.

What then may have happened at Jamnia? Nothing is known for certain. According to the Talmud and Mishnah, the canonicity of Ezekiel, Proverbs, Song of Solomon, and Esther was discussed by the scholars living in the city.[29] It seems preferable to conclude with the late Merrill F. Unger that whatever may have transpired, "official sanction (i.e., canonization) did *not* create public opinion. It merely confirmed it."[30]

With these considerations in mind we believe that the book of Ruth, as with any other portion of Scripture, would have been recognized as sacred as soon as it was written. That being the case, we can approach the text and investigate the theme of the book unencumbered by doubts raised by negative biblical criticism.

THE HEART OF THE MATTER

The confusion surrounding the date of the composition of Ruth has carried over into, and obscured, its purpose. Those who hold to a postexilic date see the book as a polemic against the supposedly harsh, authoritarian practices of Ezra and Nehemiah. Others pick up on the repeated emphasis of Ruth as a Moabitess and see in the book a "tract for the times," rebuking Judah's exclusivism. A large number of scholars believe that the whole book existed for the sole purpose of supplying Israel with David's genealogy. A significant number, however, who espouse a negative approach to biblical criticism deny the authenticity of 4:17-22.

An insignificant number of writers believe that Ruth was written as a midrash on a Bethlehem fertility-cult myth in which Elimelech represented the dying God, Naomi the mother-goddess, and Ruth her devotee.[31]

Still others believe the central point of the story to be loyalty within the family, or the friendship of two women, or to extol the providence of God. These will all be dealt with as space permits; suffice it to say that there seems to be confusion between the singular purpose of the book and its many subordinate themes. A work of literary merit can have only one central theme even though many important lessons may be gleaned from it. Oswald Loretz rightly observed:

> Exegesis has been thus far unable to supply a completely satisfactory answer to the most important question concerning the book of Ruth: what is its basic spirit or purpose? When one examines the literature that has appeared on Ruth, and takes special notice of the sections dealing with the book's author, he soon realizes how divided are the opinions of exegetes on this question. Thus, the opinion has been expressed that the book of Ruth is essentially a product of the storyteller's art.[32]

IN PRAISE OF RHETORIC

Richard Moulton was outspoken in his praise of the composition of Ruth: "So delicate in its transparent simplicity [is this book], that the worst service one can do the story is to comment on it."[33] To comment adequately upon so perfect a literary product is impossible, but to expound its theme is not an option. Its truth must be unraveled, understood, and shared, or else we will suffer the consequences of our neglect.

But how are we to understand this story? Is it a folktale, a pleasing pastoral idyll with little or no factual basis? Jack Sasson has recently propounded a theory that deals with the literary genre of Ruth. He says, "On the assumption that literature is never created in a vacuum, literary critics of the past century have begun to identify patterns in order to isolate narrative elements common to a wide variety of literature. Such enterprises were essentially reductionistic even as they were integrative and holistic."[34]

Sasson then compares various schools of literary thought. He finally advocates a morphological approach based upon the syntagmatic analysis of the structuralist school. His acceptance of the character-and-development of the plot necessitated by this viewpoint—one demanding a villain, a donor-helper, a sought-for person, the sought-for person's father, a dispatcher, a hero, and a false hero—imports to the narrative characters and elements from fiction that are totally foreign to the story. We may, therefore, dismiss his theory without further comment.

Among those scholars who appreciated the literary excellence of Ruth was S. R. Driver. He observed, "The narrator manifestly takes delight in the graceful and attractive details of his picture. His principal characters are amiable, God fearing, courteous, unassuming; and all in different ways show how a religious spirit may be carried unostentatiously into the conduct of daily life."[35] But even though we may praise the literary excellence of the writer of this book, plainly the story involves more than perfection of form.

A WAY OF LIFE

Driver's observation has led several writers to believe that the central theme or purpose of the book of Ruth is the exemplary conduct of the leading characters: Naomi, Ruth, and Boaz.

Some students of Scripture point out that the story begins and ends with Naomi (1:6ff.; 4:14-17) and believe that she is the central figure.[36] Others regard the theme as being a story of two women.[37] Still others see the book as descriptive of ideal widowhood.[38]

I. Bettan sees the all-embracing theme of the book as the law of humankindness that transcends national boundaries.[39] Leland Ryken takes this theme even further and shows how Ruth's love for Naomi led to her marriage to Boaz so that she could fulfill her duty to her mother-in-law.[40]

Keil and Delitzsch link the theme of exemplary conduct with the genealogy that concludes the book and, by quoting K. A. Auberlen and blending their thoughts with his, affirm:

> "The book of Ruth contains, as it were, the inner side, the spiritually moral background of the genealogies which play so significant a part even in the Israelitish antiquity;" so much is unquestionably true, that the book contains a historical picture from the family life of the ancestors of David, intended to show how the ancestors of this great king walked uprightly before God and man in piety and singleness of heart, and in modesty and purity of life. "Ruth, the Moabitish great-great-grandmother of David, longed for the God and people of Israel with all the deepest earnestness of her nature, and joined herself to them with all the power of love; and Boaz was an upright Israelite, without guile, full of holy reverence for every ordinance of God and man, and full of benevolent love and friendliness towards the poor heathen woman. From such ancestors was the man descended in whom all the nature of Israel was to find its royal concentration and fullest expression."[41]

G. Campbell Morgan enlarges upon this theme by claiming that there are two permanent values to be found in this short story: (1) the secrets of saintship, for God is the sufficiency of trusting souls, and (2) the values of saintship, in that trusting souls are the instruments of God. He continues:

> A saint is a person separated to the will of God. Ruth and Boaz lived the life of saintship in circumstances of the utmost difficulty, finding their sufficiency for such a life in God.
>
> Ruth was a Moabitess, of an accursed race . . . [who] came back with Naomi

into poverty, and to a people who in all probability were hostile to them both. Thus the saintship of Ruth was in spite of difficulties, and flourished amid circumstances calculated to discourage her.

Boaz lived amid people of privilege in times of degeneracy . . . he was a mighty man of wealth, and consequently able to procure whatever would contribute to the case of his material existence. That condition is always perilous to a life of faith.[42]

Morgan summarizes the character of Ruth and Boaz in the following way: "Ruth was a woman capable of love, characterized by modesty, of fine gentleness, of splendid courage; a woman in all the grace and beauty of womanhood. Boaz was a man of integrity, of courtesy, of tender passion, of courage; a man in all the strength and glory of manhood."[43]

These viewpoints have much to commend them. We must ask, however, Is that what God intended to reveal in and through this brief story? Is human character the central theme of the book, or merely one of its lessons?

Keil and Delitzsch believe that the central theme is the link between the past and the future. They state with confidence, "The meaning and tendency of the whole narrative is brought clearly to light. The genealogical proof of the descent of David from Perez through Boaz and the Moabitess, Ruth (chap. iv. 18-22), forms not only the end, but the starting-point, of the history contained in the book."[44]

UNRESOLVED TENSION

I believe that the concluding section to this short story is authentic, even though many reputable scholars feel that it constitutes a later addition.[45] It is somewhat ironic, therefore, to find some "liberal" critics affirming the genuineness of the last paragraph (though assigning the book a late date), whereas many of their colleagues deny its authenticity, claiming that the genealogy was copied from 1 Chronicles 2:12-15 by an editor.

A. Jepson stresses the comfort the genealogy brings and shows how hopelessness was turned to hope and then to triumphant assurance as Ruth gave birth to Obed.[46] R. Hals states that "the story has a theological purpose which pervaded the entire book, namely, to bear witness to God's hidden control of history by tracing his hand in the ancestry of David."[47]

But is that all we are to understand from our study of this exquisite piece of literature? Would anyone have taken the trouble to write an account of such obscure people if all he intended to do was record a genealogy for posterity? Leon Morris rightly observes, "The genealogy appears rather as an appendix than as a climax."[48]

How then are we to understand this pastoral story? A number of other suggestions have been made, which we attempt to summarize below.

SEEDS OF CORRUPTION

Those who see in the book of Ruth a protest against the supposedly rigid conditions enforced by Ezra and Nehemiah,[49] or the evils of Athaliah's reign, build their case largely upon the fact that Ruth is frequently referred to as "the Moabitess" (1:4, 22; 2:2, 6, 11-13, 21; 4:5, 10). Their theories are conditioned by their dating of the book (after the exile if written against Ezra and Nehemiah,[50] or during the latter part of the divided monarchy if directed against the practices of Athaliah[51]).

B. Vellas succinctly rebuts the case for the former view: "A book which was written in those troubled times of Ezra and Nehemiah, as a protest against those men, could not possess that beautiful atmosphere and those idyllic surroundings which, so skillfully, the author of Ruth creates, nor could it be possible to possess an unforced, serene and calm tone of style."[52]

Likewise, the belief that the book was written as a polemic against the evils of Athaliah's reign has to create from the history of those times a context in which to fit the story. But when that has been done the tenor of the book refuses to accommodate itself to that era.

UNASSIGNED FREQUENCY

Some Jewish interpreters see in the book of Ruth a tract written to promote religious zeal. Ruth the Moabitess is held up as an example of the perfect proselyte.[53] D. Harvey writes, "The emphasis of the book is not so much on Ruth's devotion to her mother-in-law, as on Ruth's acceptance in Israel in spite of her foreignness."[54]

The emphasis of the book, however, does appear to be placed on Ruth's avowal of loyalty to her mother-in-law (1:16-17); her willingness to support Naomi (chap. 2); and devotion, even to the extent of marrying a kinsman and bearing a child for Naomi when it was freely acknowledged that she could have had any man of her choosing in Bethlehem (3:10-13).

If we are to see anything in Ruth's conduct, it would be her love for and kindness to Naomi—kindness above and beyond conventional duty. That has led one rabbinic commentator to believe that the book teaches "how great is the reward that accrues to those who perform kindly deeds" (*Midrash Rabbah*, Ruth 2:14).

The theme of familial responsibility, therefore, would seem to warrant further consideration.

THE COST FACTOR

Those who believe that Ruth was designed to promote a resurgence of interest in levirate marriages stress the conduct of Boaz, who performed this rite even though he was not under legal obligation to do so. They emphasize his magnanimity, whereas his unnamed kinsman refused to marry Ruth, probably because of the financial cost involved in maintaining both her and Naomi.

Vellas, who dates the book in the postexilic period, sees the writer stressing the sacredness of family bonds in an age when, as Vellas believes Malachi 3:24 shows, those bonds were being relaxed.[55] J. P. Hyatt accepts that thesis and argues for a wider interpretation and application of levirate marriages.[56] H. H. Rowley is a little more cautious. He agrees that the story of Ruth's marriage is generally linked with the issue of levirate marriage, but admits that "this is not strictly a case of levirate marriage, since Boaz is not a brother-in-law."[57]

Although levirate marriage is illustrated in Genesis 38 (which antedates the time of Moses), the custom receives specific legislative significance in Deuteronomy 25:5-10. Driver, however, rejects all thought of levirate marriage and states that Boaz "purchased" Ruth.[58]

In light of those distinctions it seems preferable to refrain from building too much upon so tenuous a foundation.

THE REWARD OF THE RIGHTEOUS

Closely associated with the relationship of the historical and cultural approach to the book of Ruth is a view that develops the writer's thought around the ideas of emptiness and fullness. This approach to the theme of Ruth is both literary and psychological in its scope. In chapter 1, for example, we are introduced to a family enduring the hardship created by continuous famine. They migrate to Moab and there Naomi's husband dies. As the writer reminds his readers, she is bereft. Later on her sons die, and we are told that now she is bereft of her husband and her two sons. Naomi, however, hears that the Lord has visited His people in giving them bread. Here the advocates of this approach believe the author introduces the theme of fullness. "And they came to Bethlehem at the beginning of the barley harvest" rounds out the cycle.

The succeeding sections of Ruth, however, do not lend themselves as clearly or as readily to the motif of emptiness and fullness, even though hunger is present and Ruth (with help from Boaz) fends for herself and returns heavy-laden to her mother-in-law (chap. 2).

Chapter 3 has even less of the emptiness and fullness motif, although it does end with Boaz's words to Ruth, "Do not go empty to your mother-in-law" (3:17).

Chapter 4 takes on the note of triumph and celebration. It also turns the spotlight back on Naomi, for she takes Obed and becomes his nurse.[59]

Overall we are left with the impression that in this view of emptiness/fullness, Western patterns of plot development are being imposed upon an Eastern story. The result is rather like trying to force one's foot into a shoe that, for all its good appearance, is of the wrong size.

Of a similar nature is the theory that the theme surrounds the continuance of a family and the prolongation of its name. In this view, Elimelech's line was threatened with extinction. Naomi was past child-bearing years; the outlook was hopeless. Through the wife of one of Elimelech's deceased sons a son is born into the home, and the child is reckoned to Naomi. In time he becomes the grandfather of David—an event so momentous as to insure the family endless succession and renown.[60] Those who hold this view emphasize the repeated references to Elimelech (eg., 2:3; 4:9, 10) and that God in His mercy has not withdrawn His lovingkindness from the living and the dead (cf. 2:20).

There is much historical validity to this approach, but the question remains, Is the importance of the perpetuation of the family the key theme of the book? If so, then what long-lasting lesson are we to learn from it?

It seems preferable to conclude with W. Rudolph that "Ruth, like the major part of the Old Testament literature, does not speak of men but of God; its purpose is not that we should admire a gallery of noble people, but that we should learn how God acts."[61] Leon Morris agrees: "This book is a book about God. He rules over all and brings blessings to those who trust Him."[62]

THE GLORY OF GRACE

In his book on the person of God, Rudolph says that the central theme of Ruth is one of extoling God's providence and lovingkindness.[63] Jepsen sees the book as implying hope.[64] Josephus, the Jewish historian, gave his reason for including the book of Ruth in his *Antiquities of the Jews:* "I was therefore obliged to relate this history of Ruth, because I had a mind to demonstrate the power of God, who, without difficulty, can raise those that are of ordinary parentage to dignity and splendor, to which he advanced David, though he were born of mean parents" (V:ix:4).

Morris responds:

> It is better to see [the book] as a tale told because it is true and because it shows something of the relationship between God and man. There is a good deal to be said for the view that the key verse is 2:12, "The Lord recompense thy

work, and a full reward be given thee of the Lord God of Israel, under whose wings thou art come to trust" (AV). That is what the book is about. It is not without its interest that the initiative is with Ruth in chapter 2, with Naomi in chapter 3 and with Boaz in chapter 4. None of them can be said to be the person about whom the book is written. But the implication throughout is that God is watching over His people, and that He brings to pass what is good.[65]

While not wishing to disagree with so competent an expositor, it seems to me as if the book of Ruth emphasizes the grace of God.

God in His grace allowed Elimelech to go to Moab to escape the famine. The temporary stay, however, became a permanent residency and in the course of time both of Elimelech's sons married Moabite women (1:1-5). Following the death of Elimelech and his sons Naomi decided to return to Bethlehem. The reason given is that she had heard that God in His grace had visited His people in giving them food (1:6).

When Naomi returned to her native village she lamented God's treatment of her. Her thoughts were all of herself and her plight (1:19-21). No mention is made of Ruth, who, as a recent convert by the grace of God, would prove to be to Naomi better than seven sons (4:15). Furthermore, God had graciously brought Naomi and Ruth back to Judah at the beginning of the barley harvest (1:22). They would not starve.

In chapter 2 Ruth went to glean in the field and happened to ask for permission to work in a section of the field belonging to Boaz. Many expositors see this incident as a further evidence of God's gracious care of her and provision for her need.

At the end of the harvest season Naomi suggested to Ruth that she lay claim to an old Hebrew custom and request Boaz to provide "rest" for her (3:9). That "rest" would be with a husband and in the home he would provide. Here again we observe something of the gracious provision of God for His people (Deut. 25:5-10).

Finally, in chapter 4 we see the foreigner Ruth—excluded from the commonwealth of Israel, an alien to the covenants of promise, without hope and without God in the world—by God's grace redeemed and accepted by the people of Bethlehem. She finds hope and security in their city, marries, bears a son, and becomes not only the great grandmother of David but also stands in the ancestral line of the Lord Jesus Christ Himself.

Keil and Delitzsch unwittingly reinforce this idea of the grace of God by emphasizing the "Messianic trait" in the genealogy of 4:18-22. Ruth was found worthy to be made the "tribe-mother of the great and pious David, on account of her faithful love to the people of Israel, and her entire confidence in Jehovah, the God of Israel."[66]

There are many lessons to be gleaned from the story of Ruth. We believe, however, that the central theme of the book and the literary purpose that best fits the content is the grace of God and the blessings of obedience to that grace.

1

THE DYNAMICS OF LIFE'S DECISIONS

(Ruth 1:1-5)

Making decisions is a complicated process. Some of the decisions we make are practical, others are theoretical; some are thrust upon us from without, others we arrive at ourselves; some are of little consequence, but others are far-reaching in their importance.

The decision-making process has been made more complicated for us by the world in which we live. A high premium is placed on being "successful," and only the "right" decisions can be expected to meet with approval. Even in Christian circles a decision will rarely be questioned if the results achieved appear to further the work we are doing.

So life and the decision-making process have come to resemble a maze. Our desire for approval, when mingled with our beliefs and values, hedges the decisions we make with doubt and uncertainty. How then are we to know what to do? Whose counsel can we trust? The views of others are often contradictory.

Many people wish they could make decisions with the ease of James Thurber's fictional character Walter Mitty. A timid and retiring person, Walter Mitty possessed a vivid imagination. He imagined himself to be fearless and resolute and possessed of the ability to size up a situation immediately and make the right decision. In that he shares a great deal in common with us in our fantasies or daydreams.

As he drove his wife to the hairdresser one afternoon, Mitty imagined himself the commander of a plane carrying vital supplies. The situation was tense; a hurricane was brewing, and the crew was scared. The supplies, however, had to be delivered. Only he could make the split-second decisions that would enable him to pilot the plane through such weather.

"Not so fast! You're driving too fast!" said Mrs. Mitty.

"Hmm?" Mitty replied, looking at his wife absent-mindedly while the roar of the engine of the imaginery aircraft he was flying faded into the remote recesses of his mind.

Mitty drove aimlessly around after leaving his wife at the hairdresser's. He passed a hospital, and once more he was transported in his imagination into a tense and difficult situation. He was now in the operating room.

"It's the millionaire banker, Wellington McMillan," whispered a pretty nurse.

"Yes," said "Dr." Mitty. "Who has the case?"

"Dr. Renshaw and Dr. Benbow, but there are two specialists here, Dr. Remington from New York and Mr. Pritchard-Mitford from London."

The patient, however, was dying.

"Coreopsis has set in," said Dr. Renshaw with mingled resignation and despair in his voice. "If you would take over, Mitty?"

"If you wish."

And once again, through his ability to size up a situation and make the right decision, Walter Mitty succeeded where others would have failed.[1]

SOURCE OF TENSION

In contrast to Walter Mitty, the decisions we make are concerned with real-life situations. Because they often have such a far-reaching effect on our lives, we need to know something of the dynamics involved in the decision-making process.

Decisions are reached when external and internal stimuli prompt us to action. We receive different kinds of data through our senses. That information triggers our thought processes. The information is filtered through our memories and integrated with our past experiences and the things we have learned. Our emotions also swing into action and provide us with either affirmation or a note of alarm. Based on the information supplied by both our minds and emotions, our wills are motivated to action.

A CASE IN POINT

In Ruth 1 we have the opportunity to study a whole range of decisions. Elimelech was faced with the prospect of economic ruin. He chose to go to Moab, and took his wife and children with him.

Though we will look specifically at the case of Elimelech, his decision is not the only one in this chapter worthy of consideration. When Elimelech died in Moab, his wife, Naomi, decided to remain there, far removed from the comfort of friends and relatives, and adjust to the problems of widowhood.

Also in Moab, Elimelech's two sons, Mahlon and Chilion, decided to marry. From the order of their wives' names it would seem as if the elder, Mahlon, married Ruth (4:10) after his younger brother had first married Orpah (note 1:4 where Ruth is spoken of as "the second" of the wives of Elimelech's sons).

The family farmed the land for about ten more years; then Mahlon and Chilion also died. Naomi's thoughts now turned homeward, but not before she had heard that the Lord had once again brought prosperity to her people.

When Naomi shared her decision with her daughters-in-law, Ruth and Orpah decided to accompany her. On the way Naomi tried hard to dissuade them from returning to Judah with her. Her situation was hopeless; their decision to go with her was much appreciated, but it was impractical and would only bring hardship upon them. Orpah was persuaded by Naomi's words and turned back. Ruth, however, persisted in her determination to go with Naomi to Bethlehem.

Each of those decisions permits us to observe how external stimuli (such as famine, death, or marriage) sets in motion each person's thought processes, and how that information was integrated with the person's perceptions and beliefs on the one hand, and feelings and desires (or drives) on the other. The result in each case was a decision that was in keeping with the individual's true nature.

ERA OF DISCONTENT

As we consider the biblical narrative, notice first of all the external pressures that give rise to our decisions. Our story begins with the word *and*,[2] thereby placing the recorded events in the mainstream of God's revelatory history.

And it came to pass [lit., and it was] in the days when the judges governed, that there was a famine in the land. And a [certain] man from Bethlehem in

Judah [lit., Bethlehem-judah] went to sojourn in the fields of Moab, he and his wife, and his two sons. And the name of the man [was] Elimelech, and the name of his wife, Naomi; and the name[s] of his two sons, Mahlon and Chilion, Ephrathites of Bethlehem in Judah. And they came to the fields of Moab and stayed there. And Elimelech, Naomi's husband, died; and she was left, she and her two sons. And they took to themselves [as] wives women of Moab; the name of the one [was] Orpah, and the name of the other [lit., second], Ruth; and they lived there about ten years. Then Mahlon and Chilion also died, both of them, and the woman was bereft [lit., left] of her two children and her husband. [1:1-5]

With simple brevity the writer begins his story by referring us to a period of Israel's history when judges "judged" God's people (Judg. 19:1; 21:25). There was no settled government in those days; everyone "did what was right in his own eyes." It was an era in which history was continually repeating itself. Following a time of walking in submission to the revealed will of God, the people of Israel would "do evil in His sight." They would apostatize and serve the licentious gods of the heathen nations around them. To chasten them, the Lord would allow the nations whose gods they were worshiping to oppress them. This would cause the Israelites great economic and emotional distress, and in their plight they would repent and turn back to the Lord. He would then raise up a judge to deliver them. The nation would enjoy the blessing of the Lord during the remainder of that judge's lifetime, but upon his death they would again turn their backs on the Lord with the result that the cycle would begin all over again (see Judg. 2:11—3:11 as an example).

PERSONAL REMINISCENCES

In the book of Ruth we turn from the oppression and strife of the period of the judges to consider the quiet, domestic life of a family in Judah. We move from the din of battle into a humble cottage in Bethlehem.[3] There we see an ordinary family, and through the events of their lives the historian helps us understand old customs as well as the pressure of unexpected events. He shows us the toiling sheepherder and then the busy reapers. He helps us to sense their cares, witness the devotion of their women to their husbands, and experience with them their sorrows. He begins at a time in their history when a famine was sweeping over the land. Such occurrences were not uncommon; earlier famines had caused Abraham and Jacob to go down to Egypt (Gen. 12 and 41-46) and Isaac to take refuge in Philistia (Gen. 26).

God in His sovereignty had promised His people Israel that if they walked in His ways He would prosper them in all areas of life (cf. Deut. 28:1-4). On the other hand, if they rebelled against Him and did not obey His word He had assured them that He would chasten them (Deut. 28:15-68). One of the means He might use to discipline their waywardness was famine[4] (Lev. 26:16, 21; Deut. 11:16-17; Ps. 105:16; Lam. 4:4-6; Ezek. 14:21). It is significant that the famine we read about in Ruth 1 extended over all the land. Even the little village of Bethlehem in Judah was affected.

Bethlehem is situated on a narrow ridge about six miles south of Jerusalem. It occupies a spur of the central mountain range that projects eastward away from the main ridge. From this favored position, the terraced slopes break away sharply to fertile fields on the north, east, and south. The terraces are admirably suited to the growth of olive and fig trees and the cultivation of vines. The valleys below are ideal for wheat and barley, and from time immemorial the hillsides farther from the village have been used for the grazing of flocks and herds. The region is so fertile that Bethlehem, ancient Ephrathah, was called "the granary" (Heb., "House of Bread").

MISCALCULATION

With this historical background before us we come to consider Elimelech's resolve to go to Moab. From his experiences, we learn something of the internal dynamics that prompt decisions.

The famine in Canaan was so severe that Elimelech (*Eli,* "my God"; *melek,* [is] "king") felt compelled to leave his country, with his surviving livestock and his family, and try to preserve his remaining wealth by immigrating for a time into Moab. Farmers are usually very attached to the soil, and it must have been only as a last resort that Elimelech chose to leave Judah for Moab.

But why go to Moab? Why not Egypt or Philistia?

During the period of the judges, Israel was continually at war with the Philistines. Going to Philistia would obviously be out of the question. And because the Philistines' border flanked the road leading to Egypt, some writers have conjectured that they harrassed those Israelites who chose to journey to "the Land of the Nile."

It seems probable, therefore, that as Elimelech saw the sheep dying in the parched valleys and heard the mournful lowing of the now-gaunt cattle (the external data received from his senses), he felt a sense of desperation come over him (his internal response).[5] For months he had hoped for some token that the famine would soon be over, but none had appeared.

He had scanned the Jordan valley, but it too lay barren beneath the relentless rays of the sun. But in the distance he could see that the hills of Moab were tinged with green.

When Elimelech could tolerate the situation no longer, he decided to take his remaining livestock to Moab. His decision was reached only after careful deliberation. Safeguards were built into it:

• He and his family would go to Moab as resident aliens (this is inherent in the Hebrew word *gur* [1:1], translated "to live" in most versions). They would not identify themselves with the people of Moab (something that would be expected of someone taking up permanent residence there).

• He would avoid the contamination of the idolatrous practices of the Moabites by living in the fields,[6] not residing in any of the cities.

• The stay in Moab would be temporary, just long enough to survive the effects of the famine in Judah.

But why was Elimelech so concerned about going to another country when other Israelites were not? The answer is most revealing. The text informs us that Elimelech was an Ephrathite.[7] Ephrathah was the ancient name of the district in which Bethlehem stood (see Gen. 35:19; 48:7; Ruth 4:11; Micah 5:2; Heb. 5:1). To be born an Ephrathite meant that Elimelech was of ancient and noble lineage. It was the equivalent of someone today coming from a well-established family in Boston, or being a third-generation resident of Charleston, South Carolina. By referring to Elimelech as an Ephrathite, the writer intends us to understand that he came from a distinguished family. He was used to being looked up to and respected in the community. He was also probably accustomed to wealth and therefore less likely to be able to withstand its loss. Fear of the loss of his wealth, and with it the imagined loss of his influence in the community, may have been a powerful motivating force behind his decision to sojourn in Moab.

In this connection Elimelech found himself in a situation similar to many today. For a variety of reasons we may decide to change jobs or move to a different part of the country. For some, the closing down of a factory, a tantalizing offer of promotion, or some other circumstance may cause them to think seriously about moving. But the problems of relocation—the selection of a suitable place to stay, the spiritual climate of the place in which they will rear their children, and the kind of husbands or wives their children may choose to marry—are all issues that must be faced squarely before a move is made. For that reason, careful thought needs to be given to the people involved in our decisions.

GRAVEN IMAGES

The people involved in Elimelech's decision included his wife, Naomi (whose name probably signifies "pleasant [one]," "lovely," or "delight-ful"), and their two sons, Mahlon (possibly derived from the Hebrew root meaning "to be weak") and Chilion (which may signify to be of "failing" [health], or "pining").[8] These names all appear in other literature of the period (specifically texts from Ras Sharma [ancient Ugarit]).

Apparently, Elimelech's household was in agreement with his plan. They did not seem to be concerned about living for a while among the descendants of Abraham's nephew, Lot. The language of the Moabites was similar to Hebrew and, by choosing to live in the "fields of Moab," they would be associating with people whose interests in farming and animal husbandry were similar to their own.

Moab is only about 40 to 60 miles from Bethlehem; the distance varies with the route taken. The closest and most easily accessible part of Moab to emigrants from Bethlehem would be the northern portion. Moab lies north of the River Arnon (modern Wadi Mōjib) and extends to a line adjacent to the upper end of the Dead Sea. This section is approximately 3,700 feet above the level of the Dead Sea and about 2,000-2,400 feet above sea level. It is well watered and relatively flat, ideal for farming and the raising of livestock.

Verse two of the narrative reveals that Elimelech and his family, after arriving in Moab, decided to *remain* there. Apparently, everything was to their liking. They sensed an acceptance on the part of the people who possibly helped them get established. New friendships were made, and their original intent of returning to Judah as soon as possible was now postponed. The text is very explicit on this point, and the change in the verb clearly indicates a change in the original plan.[9] This being the case, we learn from the story of Elimelech the subtleties of change that may undermine our decisions.

NO HIDING PLACE

Frank W. Boreham has observed that it is possible for us to "make our decisions, and then [for] our decisions to turn around and make us." He is right. In Moab, Elimelech apparently found the people tolerant of his religious beliefs, and with many of his early concerns defused and his emotional needs so evidently met,[10] he decided to remain.

The next event we read about is the death of Elimelech. No explanation is given. Was this a judgment from God for leaving the land of His appointment?

Commentators have lined up on both sides of the issue. Samuel Cox, for example, says, "Elimelech lost his life while seeking a livelihood, and found a grave where he sought a home. And, apparently, this 'judgment' fell on him at once, judgment treading on the very heels of offense [in leaving the Land of Promise]."[11]

Thomas Fuller is inclined to attribute Elimelech's passing to natural causes rather than to divine judgment. He points out:

> I have seldom seen a tree thrive that has been transplanted when it is old. The same may be seen in Elimelech; his aged body brooks not the foreign air; though he could avoid the arrows of famine in Israel, yet he could not shun the darts of death in Moab; he that lived in a place of penury, must die in a land of plenty. Let none condemn Elimelech's removal as unlawful, because of his sudden death; for those actions are not ungodly which are unsuccessful, nor those pious which are prosperous; seeing the lawfulness of an action is not to be gathered from the joyfulness of the event, but from the justness of the cause, for which it is undertaken.[12]

We ought to be cautious in applying either censure or praise where Scripture is silent. But Elimelech's sudden passing, so soon after his change in plans, does seem to indicate that evidence for the idea of judgment is not altogether lacking. With his death Naomi was left without the protection and companionship of her husband, and her two sons were deprived of the counsel and guidance of their father.

All of this brings us to consider the outcome of decision-making.

SIGNIFICANT CONSEQUENCES

Following the death of Elimelech,[13] Naomi decided to remain in Moab. She apparently shared the same values as her husband and feared the loss of her earthly possessions if she returned to Judah.

In due time Naomi's sons, having assumed the responsibilities for running their father's farm, decided to add to their emblems of manhood by marrying. Each married a Moabite woman. Mahlon's wife was Ruth (which may mean "friendship"),[14] and Chilion's wife was Orpah (which may be derived from ʿorep, "neck").[15] The text states emphatically, "and they stayed there about ten years" (1:4). Apparently neither one had any thought of returning to his homeland.

But what are we to understand by their marriages? Was it right for those Israelites to marry Moabites? Did Naomi try to dissuade them from marrying outside of their tribe?

One of the Jewish Targums says that Mahlon and Chilion "transgressed the commandment of the Lord, and took foreign wives from among the daughters of Moab." Many of the older commentators, drawing mistakenly upon Deuteronomy 23:3, are loud in their denunciations of the sins of Naomi's sons. In fairness, it should be pointed out that the verse does not prohibit marriage to Moabites (as Deut. 7:1-5 does with the inhabitants of Canaan) but only lays certain restrictions on the children of such a union.

Of far greater importance in our consideration of the whole issue of marriage is the apostle Paul's warning in 2 Corinthians 6:14 about being unequally yoked together with unbelievers. In the case of Mahlon and Chilion, however, we have no sure knowledge that their belief in *Yahweh*, the God of Israel, went any deeper than mental assent.

But what of Naomi? How did she view the marriage of her sons to those who stood apart from the covenants of her people?

Whatever may have been her reaction and however she may have tried to dissuade them, when she found that both were determined to marry Moabite women she must have accepted what she could not change. She became to her daughters-in-law the best mother-in-law they could ever have.

And so the family, now augmented by two new brides, lived happily in Moab for about ten years. But then Ruth 1:5 records, "And they also died, both of them, Mahlon and Chilion, and Naomi was bereft of her two children and her husband."

Two more graves were dug alongside that of the husband and father. The cause of death is not given in the text, and for the purpose of the story it is unimportant. The Talmud regards the passing of Naomi's sons as a punishment for leaving Judah.[16] It is sufficient for our purposes to visualize three widows, one old and two young, standing beside three graves.

We now need to turn our attention to the life-related lessons (or principles) illustrated for us in these first five verses of Ruth.

FREEDOM TO CHOOSE

One of the most prominent of those principles is the grace of God in allowing us freedom of choice. He does not relate to us as a despot. God is glorified when we make decisions in accordance with His revealed will. He realizes that we are not all alike and builds flexibility into His dealings with us; He even permits us to make certain plans and try them out.[17] This is one of the ways we learn and eventually come to approve wholeheartedly the wisdom of His will for us (cf. Rom. 12:2).

Of course, such decisions necessitate that we study God's Word and make its principles the basis of our actions. Here we are in a more privileged position than was Elimelech or Naomi or their sons. Only the writings of Moses and the book of Joshua (and perhaps the book of Job) were a part of their national heritage at that time. They did not possess copies of God's Word, so they could not read and study it for themselves. They were dependent upon the ministry of the priests, and if the priesthood was apostate (as it often was during the days of the judges), then the Word of the Lord was not taught (cf. 1 Sam. 3:1b; see also 2:12ff.).

Although God's Word specifically stated that Canaan was the place of His choosing for His people,[18] He allowed Elimelech freedom to make certain decisions. Elimelech was certainly aware of the history of his people and of their inheritance of the land, and that is why he built safeguards into his plan to go to Moab. But those safeguards did not take into account the weaknesses of human nature. The family was accepted by the Moabites and their beliefs were tolerated. That *led to a change in Elimelech's original decision, and that change evidently placed him outside the will of God.*

What should Elimelech have done; remain in Judah?

BETTER THAN A NAME

Admittedly, Judah was the place of God's appointment for Elimelech and his family. But it is too simplistic for us to say that they should have stayed in Bethlehem unless we also provide a solution to the fear that drove Elimelech to seek refuge in Moab. To "pontificate" a course of action to Elimelech ignores the inner reasons behind his decision. We place ourselves on a par with Job's comforters if we do not provide Elimelech with something strong enough to overcome his fears (see 1 Cor. 10:13).

A close examination of the passage indicates that Elimelech attributed to the famine two characteristics that properly belong to God: the power to take away his autonomy and the power to do him harm. The famine threatened Elimelech's well-being and that of his family, and had the potential to rob him of his position in the community. The famine was thus a fear-object.[19] It generated within Elimelech a fear-conflict between what he knew to be right (remaining in the land) and the possibility of preserving his possessions by going to Moab. If he were successful, he could later return to Judah with his wealth intact and be even more influential than before.

In thinking as he did, Elimelech made the mistake of equating wealth with influence. But deciding to go to Moab did not end his fears. He knew that the Moabites were a sinful people. That generated further internal conflict, and this new source of tension was only resolved when he decided on a compromise. He would avoid the cities (which had been Lot's mistake, Gen. 13:5-13; chap. 19) and live instead in the "fields of Moab." Thus, with those safeguards he was able to overcome his fear-conflicts.

But Elimelech carried about with him a testimony to the power of God, one given to him by his parents. His name signified "My God is King." Yet he failed to acknowledge God's sovereignty in the famine and did not live in submission to His will.

Did Elimelech doubt God's power and concern for him? That is often the mistake we make, and it may have been Elimelech's as well. When we begin thinking this way we fail to give the Lord the supreme position in our lives, but when we *do* acknowledge Him as our Lord we are able to commit ourselves and our temporal circumstances to Him and trust ourselves to His all-wise care.

The name that we bear as Christians ("Christ's ones"), therefore, is more than a term. It should testify to the reality of a dynamic relationship and to our confidence in Him.

Before we leave these fascinating verses, we must also consider carefully the effect of our decisions on others.

SWORD OF DAMOCLES

It seems that no matter how careful we are in making judgments and reaching conclusions, a "sword of Damocles" hangs over our heads. Someone either known or unknown to us may adversely be affected by what we do.

Fortunately for us, God's Word contains some helpful counsel. It is part of the practical counsel the apostle Paul gave to the believers in Corinth.[20] Scripture does not curtail our liberty in Christ, but it does avoid the opposite extremes on the continuum of legalism and license. We need to keep constantly in mind the influence of our attitudes and conduct on others. We may engage in practices that for us are quite legitimate; however, they may cause a person of lesser maturity to stumble. In the exercise of our liberty, therefore, we should always be motivated by true *agapē* love (the desire for the highest good for the one loved, even to the point of self-sacrifice).

Those principles from Ruth 1:1-5 are so simple yet so important. If acted upon they will prevent our ulterior motives from (1) coloring our actions, (2) distorting our decisions, or (3) unwittingly involving others in the consequences of our deeds.

2

THE PURPOSE OF GOD IN HUMAN SUFFERING

(Ruth 1:6-22)

Psychologists tell us that there are two primary relational emotions, love and fear. Of these, love is the positive emotion and has the power to overcome fear (1 John 4:8).

As we see it develop in children, love progresses through four distinct stages.[1] As infants, children feel loved when their elemental needs are met. As long as they are warm and clean and well fed, they are content. They are the center of their own little universe.

Then, as children grow older and are able to move about for themselves, restrictions are placed on them. At this stage, their idea of love is to be left alone to do what they want.

Within a few years, their sense of being loved stems from the compliments people pay them, the gifts they receive, and other ways in which they are made to feel special. This phase of their development may last well into the teen years, or even for life. At the more advanced part of this stage romantic attachment toward someone else emerges. During these years of development, children feel loved when others are giving them their undivided attention. Self, however, is still prominent. Love to them is very much a case of their desires being fulfilled, their needs being met, their plans succeeding, and their goals being attained.

To confirm the accuracy of this observation one need only spend a little time analyzing the contents of the top ten best-selling books and the leading movies being released. That will provide ample confirmation of the shallowness and self-centeredness of what is currently described as love.

With the limited models of true love in many homes and the inadequate examples of love portrayed in the media, it is no wonder that many children never progress to the fourth stage of love. Here the highest delight is derived from the giving of oneself in service to others. True love may best be described as "desiring the highest good in the one loved, even to the point of self-sacrifice."[2]

But we may ask, What does all that have to do with the book of Ruth?

The evidence of different emotions in chapter 1 is very prominent. There is Naomi's love for her daughters-in-law and their love for her, her strong insistence that they not accompany her to Judah, and their differing responses. Orpah, who loved Naomi dearly, nevertheless showed that her devotion to her mother-in-law was not to be at the expense of herself and what was best for her future. Ruth, on the other hand, loved Naomi in a self-sacrificing way and refused to be dissuaded from returning to Bethlehem with her.

RIGHT TURN ON RED

As we consider the events described in verses 6-22 and the attitudes they disclose, we must keep in mind what had taken place in the lives of those involved. Naomi, Orpah, and Ruth had recently suffered the loss of all they held dear. Death had taken their loved ones from them, and with hearts so heavy that they thought they could no longer bear the pain, the women had returned from the gravesides.[3]

The plight of a widow in those times was precarious. Young widows might stay in their father's home (cf. Gen. 38:11), but an older widow whose parents were dead was dependent upon her children for support. If they too had already died, then her situation was desperate indeed. Unless she had the benefits of wealth left her by her late husband, she was destitute. Only in marriage was there any hope of security and the possibility of a meaningful future.

CHANGING FOR TOMORROW

With these thoughts in mind, we are ready to consider the section before us. We read:

> And Naomi arose, she and her daughters-in-law, and returned from the fields of Moab, for she had heard in the fields of Moab that *Yahweh* had visited His people[4] to give them bread [i.e., food]. And she went out from the place where

she had been, and her two daughters-in-law with her; and they went in the way to return to the land of Judah. And Naomi said to her two daughters-in-law, "Go, return, each [of you] to the house of your mother.[5] May *Yahweh* deal kindly[6] with you[7] as you have done with the dead and with me. May *Yahweh* grant that you may find rest[8] each in the house of her husband." Then she kissed them, and they lifted up their voice[s] and wept. [1:6-9]

The scene described by the writer touches our emotions. The situation of the three widows was hopeless. In the extremity of her sorrow, Naomi found that her thoughts turned Godward and homeward (1:6; see also 13*b*, 21). She had heard in Moab that *Yahweh*, the covenant-keeping God of Israel, had visited His people by once again restoring prosperity to the land. Furthermore, her presence in Moab was preventing Orpah and Ruth from returning to their homes where their father or mother might arrange a suitable marriage for them.

Naomi, therefore, decided to return to Judah. The loss of her husband and her sons had come upon her as a divine rebuke (cf. 1:13*b*). She began to see God's hand in her misfortunes. She could readily discern His kindness to her people in giving them renewed prosperity, and she realized now that it was wrong for her and Elimelech to try to escape the chastening of the Lord by leaving Judah (cf. 1:20*b*). As the thought of returning to the place of God's appointment took root in her mind, we see the beginning of a work of grace being done in her heart. Naomi's thoughts were now occupied with God. She saw His hand in the circumstances of life, and felt impelled by an inner urge to go back to Bethlehem.

Naomi prepared to leave, and Orpah and Ruth accompanied her. Whether Naomi directly communicated her intention to her daughters-in-law, or whether they realized what she planned to do when they saw her place her few earthly belongings in a shawl, we have no means of knowing. We do need to realize that there is an empathy shared by those who suffer. At such times words are unnecessary. It is probable that, out of compassion for Naomi, Orpah and Ruth decided to accompany her to Judah.

As the three of them left Moab and Naomi took the path that would lead to the Jordan River, she apparently was unaware of their intention to go with her all the way to Judah. She probably surmised that they would walk along the path with her for a short distance before saying one last fond farewell.

When the three widows reached some convenient place (perhaps the boundary of a field or the ford of a river), Naomi stopped. She turned to the two women who had shared her home for the past ten years and, acknowledging their devotion both to her and to her sons, entreated them each to return to the "house of your mother."[9] Then she prayed that the Lord would bestow His grace upon them even in Moab. "May *Yahweh* deal in lovingkindness with you, as you have dealt with the dead and with me" (1:8).

The word that Naomi used to describe the One who would grant them His blessing (*Yahweh* as opposed to *Elohim*) immediately alerts us to the work of grace that God was performing in her heart. Realizing that true blessing comes only from Him, Naomi invoked His favor upon Orpah and Ruth.

The exact nature of that blessing is described as *menûḥāh*, "rest." It signifies more than cessation of worry or anxiety. *Menûḥāh* combines the idea of security with blessing (cf. Josh. 21:45 where this same word is used in a different setting). In Naomi's prayer, *menûḥāh* implies more than just marriage. It looks at the love of a husband, the comfort and security of the home he will provide, and the provision of those temporal blessings that keep one's anxieties manageable.

A POINT TO PONDER

As we look again at Naomi's words we notice how subtly she has permitted us to glimpse the kind of relationship she had with Orpah and Ruth. The word *ḥesed*, "lovingkindness," signifies the tender, compassionate, loyal attitude of each to the other.[10] Notice the word "as" in verse 8*b*. "May *Yahweh* deal in lovingkindness with you, *as* you have dealt with the dead and with me." The lovingkindness that God bears toward His people, which also forms the basis of His relationship with them, was the same kind of attitude each member of the family bore the other. It is no wonder that, having been surrounded by such a loving, kind atmosphere, Orpah and Ruth wished to go with Naomi to Judah.

Theologically, *ḥesed* describes God's dealings with us. This is best illustrated in Exodus 34:5-8 where He describes Himself and explains to the assembled Israelites what they may expect from Him. By the impartation of grace, we may demonstrate the same loving concern for others. When this kind of attitude prevails in a home, bitterness, retaliation (verbal as well as physical), criticism, and all forms of conduct that tear at relationships are excluded.

WINDS OF AUTUMN

As Orpah and Ruth heard Naomi telling them to return to their mothers' homes, they were filled with sorrow. The loss of their husbands had brought them enough calamity; the thought of parting with their beloved mother-in-law was too much for them to bear. Together they gave expression to their feelings.

The text then reveals something of Orpah's and Ruth's passionate regard for Naomi. Of their own accord and with no collusion, they said, "No,[11] we will return with you to your people."

The words were nobly spoken and their sentiment was sincere. But Naomi realized how impossible it would be for two Moabite widows to find acceptance and any form of employment among her people. Orpah and Ruth were young and could well remarry in their own land. Naomi was too old still to entertain the prospect of bearing children;[12] she also was in no position to provide a comfortable home for any dependents. In addition, Naomi knew of her people's pride of race and their dislike for Moabites, which had resulted from Israel's past association with Moab (cf. Num. 20:18-21; Deut. 23:4). So she lovingly yet firmly said to them:

> "Turn back, my daughters; why should you go with me? Have I still sons in my womb that they should be [to] you for husbands? Return, my daughters, go; for I am too old to be [married] to a husband. If I should say, 'There is hope for me'; even [if] I should be [married] to a husband tonight, and even [if] I should bear sons;[13] would you wait for them[14] until they grow up?[15] Would you endure not to be [married] to a husband? No, my daughters, for it is much more bitter for me than [it is] for you that the hand of *Yahweh* has gone out against me." [1:11-13][16]

Naomi has been severely criticized for suggesting that Orpah and Ruth return to Moab.[17] Some believe that Naomi should have constrained both her daughters-in-law to accompany her to Judah, for there they would have come under the influence of the truth and may even have come to believe in the one true God. To suggest that they return to a culture permeated by paganism and idolatry of the worst kind was to condemn their souls.

Cox, however, has paraphrased the intent of Naomi's words. He writes,

> If we would understand the scene, and especially the stress laid on these young widows finding new husbands, we must remember that in the East of antiquity, as in many Eastern lands to this day, the position of an unmarried woman, whether maid or widow, was a very unhappy and perilous one. Only in the house of a husband could a woman be sure of respect and protection. Hence the Hebrews spoke of a husband's house as a woman's *menuchah*, or "rest"— her secure and happy asylum from servitude, neglect, license. It was an "asylum" of honour and freedom that Naomi desired for Orpah and Ruth. But as she had to explain to them in Moab, would be fast closed against them in Judah. In marrying them her sons had sinned against Hebrew law. That sin was not likely to be repeated by Israelites living in their own land. Yet how is Naomi to tell them of this fatal separation between the two races? How is she to make these loving women aware that, if they carry out their resolve to go with her,

they must resign all hope of honour and regard?

She discharges her difficult task with infinite delicacy. They, of course, had no thought of marrying any sons that might hereafter be born to the widowed Naomi. Such a thought could not possibly have entered their minds. Why, then, does Naomi lay such emphasis on the utter unlikelihood of her having sons and of their waiting for them even if she could have them? Simply to convey to them that, if they went with her, *they would have no hope but in herself*. What she meant was: "I know and love you: and, had I sons, I would take you with me, that in their homes you might find the asylum every woman needs and craves. But I have none, nor am I likely to have any, nor could you wait for them if I had. And, outside my household, there is no prospect for you; for the men of Israel may not take to wife daughters of Moab. Alas, it is more bitter for me to tell you this than for you to hear it. It is harder for me than for you that we must part. But the hand of the Lord has gone out against me. I have no hope for the future. I must walk my darkened path alone. But you, you may find an asylum with the people of your own race. *Your* future may be bright. You will at least have one another. Go, then, and return each to her mother's house."[18]

Naomi's words had a profound effect upon her daughters-in-law. As the reality of their situation gripped them, Orpah and Ruth sensed more fully than before the desperate plight they were in. They gave way once more to loud weeping (1:14).

PARTING OF THE WAYS

Naomi had previously taken the initiative by kissing her daughters-in-law. Now it was Orpah who kissed Naomi. It was a kiss of farewell; their relationship was at an end.[19] As Robert A. Watson has pointed out, Orpah was a kind of woman who was worldly-wise.[20] To her the arguments of Naomi were persuasive. She saw the future as Noami had painted it. In Moab she had some slender hope of future happiness. On the other hand, to go with Naomi to Judah would mean only ostracism, grief, and misery. Therefore she kissed Naomi goodbye and took the road leading to her mother's home.

There can be no doubt that when all was going well in Naomi's household, Orpah loved her kind, considerate mother-in-law. Naomi brought happiness and stability to the home. But when the strong winds of adversity had removed all buffers from her, Orpah thought solely of herself and departed.

NEW VALUES VERSUS OLD TRADITIONS

Although we should not reproach Orpah for her decision, the biblical writer uses Orpah's departure to highlight the steadfast love and devotion of Ruth. Ruth did more than embrace Naomi, she clung to her (1:14*b*). To this point Ruth had stood in the shadows. Now, however, she emerged from obscurity and revealed a love for and devotion to her mother-in-law that is at once beautiful and inspiring.

But as Ruth and Naomi looked at the retreating figure of Orpah, Naomi disengaged Ruth's arms from around her. "Look," she said, "your sister-in-law has returned to her people and to her gods. Return after your sister-in-law" (1:15).

Naomi's words were simple and direct. Hers was a self-sacrificing love, for it is certain that if she had thought only of herself she would have delighted in the company of both of her daughters-in-law. Naomi, however, had dealt honestly with them by aptly describing the kind of situation they would face in a strange land.

But why did Naomi mention that Orpah had returned "to her gods"?

Might Naomi have said it to cause Ruth to realize the spiritual realities that were latent in her own decision? Did Naomi sense in this young woman an emerging sensitivity to spiritual things that was missing in Orpah? We cannot be sure. What is important to notice is that Naomi permitted each woman to make her own decision. She might weigh the issues for them, but in the final analysis each acted upon her own initiative.

Having before her the example of Orpah, Ruth nevertheless chose to remain with Naomi. In a spirit of true devotion, she said: "Do not press me to leave you, to return from [following] after you; for where you go, I will go, and where you stay, I will stay; your people [shall be] my people, and your God [will be] my God. Where you die, I will die, and there I will be buried. Thus[21] may *Yahweh* do to me, and more so, if [anything but] death[!] parts me and you" (1:16-17).

Rhetoricians have not been able to improve on the eloquence of Ruth's statement. With an astounding economy of words she declared her loyalty to Naomi, her willingness to be numbered among Naomi's people, and her submission to Naomi's God. In a single statement, she separated herself from her former god(s).[22] Her knowledge of *Yahweh* was not well-developed but it was real, and she willingly acknowledged His sovereignty over her life from that moment forward.

CRUCIAL CHOICE

Ruth's love for Naomi was deep and mature. It was the self-sacrificing kind that finds its highest delight in giving itself in the service of others.[23]

As we weigh Ruth's words in verses 16 and 17, it is difficult not to see that one of the purposes of God in human suffering is to bring people to a personal knowledge of His saving grace. Often an individual can trace his spiritual awakening to some form of adversity. We find that Ruth had been awakened to spiritual realities through the death of her husband. When faced with this crucial choice, she boldly declared her submission to the authority of Naomi's God. Furthermore, she did not look upon Naomi's God as a tribal deity who might rule only a certain territory, but acknowledged His power (in the event she might break her promise) wherever she might be. In addition, she did not use the general name for God, *Elohim,* but referred to Him by His most revered name, *Yahweh.*

The importance of a personal decision has been underscored by Watson: "In religion there is no escape from personal decision; no one can drift to salvation with companions or with a church. . . . The supreme nature of religion and its unique part in human development are seen here, that it demands high and sustained personal effort."[24]

As with many before and since, Ruth was influenced in her decision, not by smooth words or manipulative devices, but by the example and influence of another.

SENSITIVE ISSUES

The last section of chapter 1 is likewise replete with evidence of the grace of God:

> And when Naomi saw that Ruth was determined [lit., "had made herself strong," i.e., was firmly resolved] to go with her, she ceased trying to persuade her. So they went, both of them, until they came to Bethlehem. And it was, when they came to Bethlehem, that all [who were in] the city were stirred because of them. And the women said, "Is this Naomi?" And Naomi said to them, "Do not call me Naomi ["pleasant"], call me Mara ["bitter"], for *Shaddai*[25] [the Almighty] has dealt very bitterly with me. I went out full, and *Yahweh* has brought me back empty.[26] Why do you call me Naomi, since *Yahweh* has witnessed against me [lit., "has eyed me"], and *Shaddai* has done evil to [i.e., "has afflicted"] me?" [1:18-21]

THE WELCOME

The journey back to Judah is not described. Because it would have taken two or three days and involved sleeping in a field or a cave at night, Naomi must have been glad to have Ruth with her. Even though their situation was hopeless, humanly speaking, God is the Defender of the destitute and the Helper of the poor. Now that Naomi was returning to the place of blessing, she had hope that despite all indications to the contrary, He would help her.

As they neared Bethlehem the women[27] came out to see who was climbing the slopes to their village. They recognized Naomi, and with delight welcomed back an old friend.[28] As they clamored around her, showering her with questions, Naomi gave expression to the deep-seated hurt in her heart. She had left Bethlehem with a husband and sons. Her desire then was to preserve her material wealth. In Moab she had lost her family, and as a result life had now become empty.

AT ROCK BOTTOM

Naomi's reaction is not unnatural. We too are apt to blame God for our misfortune when we suffer. "If He is who He claims to be," we reason, "then why did He not prevent this from happening to me?"

In Naomi's case, however, she was also conscious of having done wrong (cf. 1:13b, 20b, 21b), and she viewed the loss of her husband and sons as God's punishment for her sins. That is why she used the name *Shaddai*. He is all-powerful. He has done to her as He wished. Against Him she was powerless.[29]

At times like that it is hard for us to understand the purpose God may have in our suffering. We see the grace of God at work in Naomi's life, as He restored her sense of values. In her own words, "I went out full." She had left Judah to preserve what she valued most. In Moab she had come to realize life's true values. She had not realized how blessed she was in Bethlehem, even with the famine and the threatened loss of their earthly possessions. But now she had come to realize the true worth of human relationships.

This truth is highlighted in the experience of a woman who sought an attorney to represent her in a divorce suit against her husband. After listing the reasons she wanted to end her marriage, and after listing the personal property she wanted assigned to her, she asked her attorney, "Will I win?"

He replied, "Mrs. Simpson, nobody wins in a divorce." Life's real values are in relationships!

One Sunday I shared this message in a church in California. A couple whom I had counseled on several occasions happened to be present. The wife had separated from her husband, but on that Sunday they were enjoying one of their frequent reconciliations. As I explained Naomi's experiences leading up to her new awareness of real values I prayed earnestly that the Holy Spirit would apply the Word of God to the lives of that couple.

After the service, the couple came up to me as I stood on the patio greeting the worshipers. Each one threw his arms around me and hugged me. Then, with tears in their eyes, they said that the story of Naomi and how she had learned the true values in life had done more for them than all the counseling they had received.

I am glad to say that that couple is now happily reconciled. Fortunately, they learned before it was too late that life's values are to be found in the love and affection of a husband and wife, and of parents for their children.

THE TAPESTRY OF TIME

How did the women of Bethlehem receive Ruth? No one paid any attention to her. Not even Naomi mentioned her and the sacrifice she had made.

But within a few weeks Ruth would win the admiration and respect of the people (cf. 3:11b). Furthermore, for Naomi's sake she would contract a marriage with her late father-in-law's kinsman, Boaz. And later, when her son was born, those same women who ignored her would say to Naomi, "Your daughter-in-law . . . who loves you, is better to you than seven sons" (4:15).

ADVERSE WINDS

So it is that God has a purpose in allowing adversity to come into our lives. He does not forsake us or leave us to our own devices but, as William Cowper wrote, "Behind a frowning providence, He hides a smiling face." In His grace He is able

> To comfort all who mourn,
> To give to those who mourn in Zion,
> Giving them a garland [of joy] instead of ashes,
> The oil of gladness instead of mourning,
> The mantle of praise instead of the spirit of fainting.
>
> Isaiah 61:2c-3

Perfect Timing

As he concludes this section of his story, and as a further evidence of God's grace, the inspired writer both summarizes what has happened thus far and prepares us for what is to follow. "And Naomi returned, and with her Ruth the Moabitess, her daughter-in-law, who returned from the fields of Moab; *and they came to Bethlehem at the beginning of the barley harvest*" (1:22, italics added).

Years before, when God had given His people the laws that were to govern their lives in Canaan, He had made specific provision for the poor. He had built into the Mosaic legislation a decree that at harvest time the poor should be allowed to glean ears of grain that were dropped by the reapers during the harvesting process.

In accordance with God's gracious nature, and as evidence of His concern for Naomi, He brought Naomi and Ruth back to Bethlehem "at the beginning of the barley harvest [April/May]." They would not go hungry!

THE UNSEEN HAND

At this point we need to consider for a moment the One who was present in all of the events that transpired. He orchestrated everything from Naomi's hearing of the prosperity of her people to the return of Naomi and Ruth at the very beginning of the harvest.

Many of us have defective views of God. Depending on our outward circumstances, we may view Him as a "cosmic policeman" who (at best) will "blow the whistle" on us if He sees us having any fun, and who always stands ready to arrest us if we do anything wrong. To others He is an "absentee landlord" who periodically and without announcement invades our lives, checks up on us, and penalizes us for all the errors of omission and commission we have made. In both of these views God is looked upon as a harsh, unreasonable deity, who is totally unsympathetic with our desires or aspirations, problems or limitations.

Others have a purely utilitarian view of God. They see Him as a "cosmic bellboy" whose responsibility it is to answer their every prayer, and come running to their aid whenever they get into trouble or have a particular need of Him. When not needed, however, He is to stay out of the way. When those who think of God in such terms find that He does not always answer their prayers or that some of their desires remain unfulfilled, they begin to doubt His involvement in their lives and wonder if He can be trusted at all. That tends to breed disillusionment and eventually the attitude, "I'll just have to get along as best I can, for God cannot be relied on to help me when I need Him."

How dramatically those false concepts of God change when we consider His lovingkindness for Naomi, Orpah, and Ruth. That does not mean that He did not deal in grace with Mahlon and Chilion. He did. He gave them ten years in which to return to Bethlehem. When as the leaders of the family they continued to flout His wishes, He began to accomplish His plan (see 4:13, 18-22; Matt. 1:5-6, 17) in some other way.

Of course, Naomi was unaware of the far-reaching effects of her decision to return to Judah, and so was Ruth. The realities of life and their personal needs crowded out of their minds the broader scope of God's purpose for them and their descendants. But God demonstrated His loving concern for Naomi by leading her back to the place of blessing.

There He would amply reward her. And there too Ruth, who had come to trust under the shadow of *Yahweh*'s wings, would find His blessing in ways that would seem impossible.

The grace of God also led Naomi to acknowledge her former sin (cf. 1:13*b*, 20*b*, 21*b*). Her confession, accompanied by a cathartic expression of her feelings, removed the barriers that had been erected between herself and God. She still felt her loss acutely but, as we shall see in chapter 2, her former jubilant spirit would soon rise above the winds of adversity that had blown over her soul.

The grace of God also led to Ruth's conversion, so blessing was already beginning to attend Naomi's obedience. And on the long road home, Naomi had the benefit of Ruth's companionship as she retraced the steps she and Elimelech had taken a little more than a decade before.

The women of Bethlehem clamored around Naomi on her arrival. They saw alterations in her appearance, but they were unconscious of those changes in themselves. The saddest part of all was that they made no response to her sorrow. As Taylor has observed,

> Had she come back with pomp and glory and riches they would have made much of her; for the world always fawns upon prosperity, and those who need least of its attentions get the most. But Naomi's account of her circumstances seems to have dampened the ardor of the welcome given her by her old neighbors. None of them invited her home, or offered her hospitality. She was too poor now to be acknowledged in that way; and after the first expressions of surprise at her appearance, they let her severely alone.[30]

But God had not forgotten her, nor would He fail to provide for her temporal needs. His timing of her return was perfect (1:22*b*).

The manifestations of God's grace so evident in this story should prove an antidote to pride in prosperity and to despondency in adversity. From His working in the life of Naomi we should learn to gladly trust God's sovereign will for us even when all our human inclinations might lead us to a different conclusion.

3

WHAT TO DO WHEN LIFE TUMBLES IN

(Ruth 2:1-7)

In his book *How to Prosper During the Coming Bad Years,* Howard Ruff shares with his readers his experience of life's adversity.

It was November; Thanksgiving was over. He and his family had been painfully reminded of the loss of their youngest son only five months earlier. Now shop windows were reminding people that there were only four weeks until Christmas.

On that particular morning Ruff had been called to his office for a special meeting. The past year had been a difficult one. A strike had virtually paralyzed his business. At last, however, there had been a turn for the better, and the future looked promising. Ruff went to his office confident that he would receive help and advice from the people who managed the national company with which he had a speed-reading franchise.

But instead of the needed assistance, Ruff found his franchise canceled. His banker froze all his assets, and he found himself on the sidewalk with $11.36 in his pocket. He was declared bankrupt. He had no money, no job, and no unemployment insurance.

Insult was added to injury when the San Francisco Bay area newspapers carried the story of his spectacular business collapse. In addition, the Oakland Symphony Finance Committee asked for his resignation because he was an embarrassment to them.

Members of the Ruff household faced a bleak Christmas. They decided, however, that "such pain, public humiliation and grief were to be put to some positive purpose, for others, as well as themselves." Armed with this determination they tabulated their assets: a strong religious upbringing that stressed a rugged kind of independence; a sound knowledge of economics; and Howard's years of experience as an actor and singer with expertise in persuasion and communication.

With tenacity of purpose Ruff began to build a meaningful future from the traumatized pieces that remained after he hit bottom. In time he repaid all his debts, even though the insolvency forced upon him did not require him to do so. And now, ten years later, he has published books that have become national best sellers, he edits the *Ruff Times* newsletter (which provides its readers with counsel on investments), and hosts his own television talk show called "Ruffhouse."[1]

At Wit's End

Naomi and Ruth knew what it was like to be destitute, perhaps even despised and, from a human point of view, forsaken. Their welcome in Bethlehem soon faded. Poverty in that culture was regarded as a sign of God's displeasure,[2] and so Elimelech's widow, once proud and of the aristocracy, was now left severely alone with her daughter-in-law.

In Bethlehem, Naomi and Ruth returned to the cottage that in happier times had resounded to the laughter of children and where, in the cool of the evening, Naomi had sat and listened as Elimelech told her of the affairs of the day. What memories must have lingered there still! Certainly *now* she realized that to have a husband and children were evidences of God's favor; to lose them was to empty life of all that made it worth living.

A Friend in Need

Although Naomi and Ruth may have felt as if they were destitute, the inspired writer provides us with a link in the narrative that prepares us for what is to follow. He does it so subtly that we tend to pass over Ruth 2:1 without paying much attention to what it says. We need to remember that as Boaz is introduced, the two women are unaware of the part he will play in their future: "Now Naomi [had] a relative[3] of her husband, a mighty man of valor, of[4] the [extended] family of Elimelech, and his name was Boaz" (2:1).

The exact nature of the relationship between Boaz and Elimelech is not stated. Some Jewish writers believe that Boaz was Elimelech's nephew.[5] The important point is that Boaz is related to Elimelech, not Naomi. Had he been related to Naomi he would not have been able later on to perform the duty of a kinsman.

Boaz is described as a *gibbôr*, "a mighty man of valor."[6] Some translators are inclined to render this expression as if it referred to his wealth. The usage of this word in Judges 11:1 as well as in Ruth 3:11 seems to indicate that "valor" is the preferable rendering.[7] Those were troubled times, and any man might have to fight to protect his crops, herds, house, or land from the plundering raids of Bedouin or the encroachments of the local Canaanites. Their only law was "might is right" and "I am entitled to take from you whatever I can." For the present, all we need to know is that Boaz is destined to become the means whereby the grace of God is extended to Naomi.

WOMAN OF VALOR

As soon as Naomi and Ruth had made the cottage livable, Ruth took upon herself the material support of her mother-in-law.

> And Ruth the Moabitess[8] said to Naomi, "Let [me] now go to the field,[9] and glean among the ears of grain after him in whose eyes I shall find favor."[10] And Naomi said to her, "Go, my daughter." So Ruth went, and came [to the field], and gleaned in the field after the reapers; and she happened by chance[11] upon the portion of the field [belonging to] Boaz, who [was] of the family of Elimelech. [2:2-3]

Although Ruth had been in Bethlehem only a short time, she had already looked about her to see what she could do to support Naomi. She was proactive, not reactive. She did not wait for something to happen, but took the initiative. In that she sets a good example for those in a similar situation.

Different people respond to adversity and the painful reverses of life in different ways. Some become passive and expect everything to be done for them. As their dependency upon others increases, they also tend to cling to them for support.

Others, according to William Hulme in his book *Creative Loneliness,* become self-centered. They indulge themselves.[12] Either for the sake of security or out of a desire to believe that someone wants them, they may engage in promiscuous sexual relationships (in contrast to Ruth in 3:10*b*).

Relatively few, however, are able to make the adjustments of culture and status, which Ruth made with ease, and also undertake the support of another.

All of this was not lost on the author of the book. That is why at the beginning of chapter 2 he reminds us that Ruth was a foreigner. She was a stranger in a strange land.

"But what," we may ask, "is required of a person if he or she is to surmount the adversities that invariably come one's way?"

Modern research has identified five characteristics that are of fundamental importance to each of us if we are to triumph over the vicissitudes of our human existence and lead happy, effective, fulfilled lives. These criteria are:

• A sense of personal autonomy
• Our sexuality (i.e., how we think of ourselves as men or women)
• Our internalized sense of morality
• Our career choice
• Our hope for the future[13]

We will consider each of these and seek to ascertain from the biblical record how they apply to the heroine of our story.

A TIME FOR BOLDNESS

Without waiting for any prompting Ruth asked Naomi, "Let me now go to the field and glean." She was appropriately assertive and, at the same time, willingly subordinate to her mother-in-law. As a stranger she naturally looked to Naomi for guidance in matters of local custom. But this did not make her passive. Her proposed solution to their very evident need was indicative of her freedom of thought and ability to come to a decision.

Then notice that in seeking a place to begin gleaning, Ruth went to the field where the reapers were. She was unaware that God in His grace was leading her to "the portion of the field belonging to Boaz." Her plan was to find someone who would allow her to glean. She saw a foreman supervising the reapers and asked permission to gather up the grain that had fallen to the ground.[14]

The manner in which Ruth spoke to the foreman showed that she did not presume on his favor or on her rights as an alien. The law specifically stated that the poor and strangers were to be allowed to glean in the fields at harvest time (Lev. 19:9f.; 23:22; Deut. 24:19). Ruth, however, was unobtrusive. She *requested* permission to glean in between the sheaves. If denied permission, she apparently was prepared to persevere with her quest until some other foreman gave his consent (2:2). Such resilience is an outgrowth of a well-balanced personality and shows a well-developed sense of autonomy.

In most cultures an individual's sense of autonomy is developed prior to his leaving home. Skills are cultivated that prepare him to function and be self-supporting. Generally speaking, physical maturation is important to proper autonomy, for certain functions require a measure of strength, coordination, and endurance.

In addition, the process of identification and the accompanying internalization of values (which will be discussed below) assist him to adopt an appropriate and comfortable style of behavior. One aspect of this behavior is seen in his independence of action.

Autonomy also necessitates the development of mental and emotional maturity. As a person grows he acquires a certain amount of knowledge. This is shown in job preferment (based on one's experience of success), problem-solving ability, and planning for the future. Emotional maturity, however, is also needed. This often takes the form of being able to establish lasting relationships outside the home, possessing the capacity for intimacy, and letting go the last strings of dependence upon parents.

As we compare these broad principles of personal autonomy to Ruth's experience, we find that of her own volition she left her father and mother and the country of her birth for a land that was previously unknown to her (2:11). Such an act required considerable personal maturity.

As a newcomer to Bethlehem, Ruth faced a problem. How would she support Naomi? She solved the problem by doing what she could as first one opportunity and then another presented themselves. Her long-range planning is perhaps best seen in chapter 3, where she asked Boaz to marry her so that Naomi would be cared for. Her actions throughout these chapters reflected her emotional maturity, for she was always thinking of others, not of herself.

Further investigation reveals that a person's autonomy is intimately connected with the way he views himself as an individual; in a word, a person's *sexuality*—how a man thinks of himself, and how a woman thinks of herself.

THE ISSUE OF SEXUALITY

Mature sex-role identity may be traced back to one's relationship with his parents, and particularly the parent of the same sex. From their fathers boys learn what is required of men, the social expectations or standards set for them, and how they are to relate to women. From their mothers girls learn what women are like, how to perform the duties that fall within the domain of a woman, and how they should relate to men.

Later on, both boys and girls develop heterosexual relationships and experience the pressure for mature sex-role behavior. At this stage young men are expected to give promise of being able to hold a steady job and provide for a family, and young women are expected to develop discrete patterns of behavior and acquire those skills that will help them become good wives and mothers or pursue a career themselves.

In Ruth's case we have good reason to believe that her ten-year marriage to Mahlon was a happy one. Although they had no children, she gave every evidence of being the kind of wife who was loving and affectionate toward her husband, and was appropriately supportive of him. Now, however, as a widow and alien Ruth was in an invidious position. The work she chose to support herself and Naomi was not without its hazards. As Cox has pointed out, the "reapers were apt to be vicious and rude," especially to strangers (2:9a). "All through this chapter we see that Ruth ran a great risk [of sexual abuse]"[15] (see also 2:22).

Two kinds of people are most liable to sexual harassment. They are those who flaunt their sexuality, and those who are shy and retiring. Only a woman who is comfortable in her role as a woman can steer a middle course, be noticed, and yet escape molestation. We notice that the young man who was placed over the reapers was sufficiently attracted to Ruth to watch her (2:7).

From all that is revealed to us in the book, we gather that Ruth was winsome and possessed that feminine mystique that made her attractive to others. Yet she did not flaunt her sexuality or use it to gain the ends she sought. She appeared to be confident in her role as a woman and free from any need to draw attention to herself. Further evidence of her attractiveness comes from Boaz himself (3:10b). He said that she could have had her pick of any of the young men of the village. They too were obviously attracted to her, but she did not encourage them.

Ruth's situation held a built-in danger. To use the biblical terminology (2:5b), she did not "belong" to any man,[16] and so she had no one to protect her. And being a foreigner from a despised race, she was very vulnerable. That is why Boaz instructed his servants not to abuse (or insult) her.

A QUESTION OF RIGHT AND WRONG

According to those students of human nature who have thoroughly researched modern man's moral development, there are three levels or stages in one's progress toward a mature sense of right and wrong.[17] These stages of development are: (1) A concern with the external consequences of one's acts and the power of those who are authority figures in our lives, (2) The maintaining of an existing rule structure with due respect for authority, and (3) A commitment of oneself to a personal or universal set of moral principles.

The growth process may be seen as a search for a set of values that will preserve one's integrity and guide one's behavior. The decisions a person makes are therefore an evidence of the moral principles to which he has committed himself.

Here it is interesting to consider Ruth's Moabite ancestry. She had a surprisingly well-defined, internalized set of standards that freed her from the fear of others' disapproval. Her conduct was not controlled by rituals, peer groups, or externalized standards of morality. All her actions give us the feeling that she was acting in complete freedom. She appears to have had a mature value system that guided her behavior and, in spite of pressures brought to bear upon her, enabled her to handle the reverses of life without violating her integrity.

Ruth's life gave evidence that she had been able to shun the licentious practices of her people and also avoid the legalism that frequently characterized the zealous Hebrew. She seemed to enjoy a life of freedom from both of these extremes. As a result she was happy in herself, joyful in her new-found faith, and ready to give of herself for the sake of her mother-in-law. No wonder people found her attractive.

LOVE'S LABOR

In addition to a sense of personal autonomy, a clearly defined sense of sexuality, and an internalized standard of morality, the choice of a career is an important part of a person's identity. It helps to determine much of his adult life-style—his daily routine, associates, and social status. It is also a direct or indirect reflection of his system of values.

When counseling young people regarding their choice of a career, I usually recommend that they keep their options open; they should evaluate possible professions in light of their personal investigation, introspection, and self-evaluation, and weigh the openings in light of their skills, temperament, values, and future goals.

Later in life when people face crises, the first thing they do when they begin to put the pieces of life back together is to consider their options. What possibilities are open to them? These may be fewer than when they were younger.

As we consider Ruth's situation, we realize that she was not permitted the luxury of too many options. Job opportunities were virtually nonexistent. Being a servant woman or, if she was still young and attractive, a prostitute, were about the only two "vocations" that widows in Old Testament times could follow.[18] Ruth was willing to take whatever menial work she could find. In her culture there were no other alternatives, except seasonal ones like harvesting.

Because God in His grace had brought Naomi and Ruth back to Bethlehem at the beginning of the barley harvest, Ruth saw the reapers going out to the field and determined to join them. Taylor writes:

> Nor was she scrupulous as to the sort of industry in which she might engage. It might be true that she had been in comfortable circumstances, and had never needed to do any kind of outdoor work while her husband lived; but she accepted the situation now, and was willing to do anything, however lowly, if only it were honest, for her own and her mother's livelihood. She did not dictate to Providence, or say that if she could get this or that she would take it, but she could never bring herself to do that other. Rather she is willing to take any honorable course that might open to her, and, as gleaning was the first that presented itself, she would take that, unless Naomi objected.
>
> It is always hard for those who have been in comfort and are reduced to destitution to bring this willinghood to take what offers, and perhaps it was easier for Ruth to act on such a determination in Bethlehem than it would have been in Moab, among those who had known her when she was better off. But in all cases, *that* is the surest way out of penury, and the sooner it is taken the shorter is the road.[19]

RAY OF HOPE

All of this brings us to consider the one ingredient that is indispensable to life—hope. People need, and in fact must have, hope. Without it there is only increasing discouragement and eventual despair.

Boaz verbalized Ruth's hope when he said, "*Yahweh* shall repay your work, and your reward shall be complete from *Yahweh,* the God of Israel, under whose wings you have come to take refuge" (2:12).

The apostle Paul too had hope in the midst of adversity. On the basis of his confidence in God's ability to undertake for His own he could write, "We are afflicted in every way, but not crushed; perplexed, but not despairing; persecuted, but not forsaken; struck down, but not destroyed; . . . we do not lose heart . . . for momentary, light affliction is producing for us an eternal weight of glory (2 Cor. 4:8-9, 16-17, NASB*).

Ruth's new faith in the one true God gave her hope as she faced the future. As she rose to meet the challenge before her, she drew upon inner resources and, as we shall see, in a few short weeks had impressed everyone in Bethlehem with her winsomeness and character (3:11*b*).

As it was with Ruth, so it is with us. Our sense of personal autonomy,

New American Standard Bible.

the way we think of ourselves, our internalized sense of morality, our career choice, and our confidence in the Lord help us face life and overcome the tensions and setbacks that are a part of everyone's experience.

FIRST IMPRESSIONS

At this juncture the biblical writer makes an abrupt change in what he has been recording. He draws our attention away from Ruth and toward Boaz:

> And behold,[20] Boaz came from Bethlehem and said to the reapers, "*Yahweh* be with you."[21] And they replied, "May *Yahweh* bless you." And Boaz said to his young man[22] set over his reapers, "Whose [is] this young woman?"[23] And the young man set over the reapers answered and said, "A young Moabitess woman[24] who returned with Naomi from the fields of Moab. And she asked, 'Please let me glean, and I will gather among the sheaves,[25] after the reapers'; and she came and has remained from [early] morning[26] until now; [except that] she sat a little while in the house." [2:4-7]

In these verses we are given

> a graphic picture of an ancient harvest scene. The field is thick with waving barley. The reapers cut their way into it with sickles, grasping the ears till their arms are full. Behind them the women gather up the armfuls and bind them into sheaves. Still farther in the rear follow the widow and stranger, who, according to the Hebrew law, have the right to glean after the reapers. The overseer is busily urging on the reapers, and granting or refusing admission to the gleaners." [Skins filled with water hang from the branch of a nearby tree, kept cool by the soft breeze. A "house" is also there in which those who are weary may rest from the glare and heat of the sun.] Here, too, under the shade of some spreading tree, men and women gather at mealtime, and are supplied with parched corn . . . which they dip in a cool and strengthening mixture of vinegar and oil and water.[27]

It is to such a scene that Boaz came. Our first impression of him is most favorable. He was gracious and cordial. In his greeting to the reapers, he showed that he was a man of keen spiritual sensitivity. He appeared to know that all blessing comes from the Lord, and he desired His blessing to be experienced by the reapers as well. He therefore greeted them in the name of the Lord.

Boaz also took a kindly interest in Bethlehem's poor who were gleaning in his field. Theirs was a backbreaking work, and a day of hard labor would yield barely enough to meet the needs of an entire family for only a few days.

The writer tacitly intimates that Boaz knew all of those in his field personally, for when he saw one whom he did not know, he inquired about her. The stranger he had noticed, of course, was Ruth. The question Boaz put to his overseer is revealing. "To whom does this young woman belong?" (2:5b). He presumed that she was married and had recently come to live in the village with her husband.

The response Boaz received is also interesting. The definite article is missing from the young man's reply as if he is implying that Ruth, being poor and not from Israel, is hardly worth noticing. We might paraphrase the young man's reply to Boaz as follows: "She's a young Moabitess; [the] one who came back with Naomi." She is also too insignificant to be identified by name.

In that single sentence the foreman has shown us a great deal about himself. He was conscious of social rank, national pride, and where everyone stood (or should have stood) in the "pecking order." He was obviously informed and for that reason the information he was able to pass on to Boaz was of value. Boaz, however, demonstrated by his actions (2:8ff.) that he did not accept his assistant's system of values.

But something else is important about the young man's response to Boaz's inquiry. Although he would have denied that Ruth was anything but a foreigner, she had made an impression on him and he had been watching her. He had even noticed when she took a brief rest under the shelter[28] that had been built for the benefit of the workers.

By little statements like these he betrayed the mixed emotions within him; and we, by our words, tend to do the same.

EASILY OVERLOOKED FACTS

The young foreman's description of the way Ruth approached him, as well as her conduct in the field, enlarges our understanding and appreciation of her. Her "Please let me glean" was phrased delicately and anticipated an affirmative answer. She was gracious and positive in her attitude. She had suffered much, but she was not depressed (2:11b). The setbacks of the past few weeks had not left her in despair. She may have been beaten down by the sheer weight of her trials, but she still had confidence in herself and in the One under whose wings she had taken refuge (2:12b). And because of her love for her mother-in-law she was determined to persevere.

Under such circumstances one's insecurities, apprehension over the future, and concern over where the next meal will come from might lead to frenetic activity. Was this true of Ruth? Let us read between the lines. Boaz's servant described her activity (2:7b). She had started early, worked diligently, and when she was tired, she had rested. Ruth was evidently sufficiently secure in herself and confident enough in the Lord not to allow her anxieties to goad her into unwarranted activity. There is no evidence in the story that fear of impoverishment drove her to the border of panic. She worked hard, and when she felt the need, she relaxed.

All of this points to Ruth's well-rounded personality. It also provides a good model for our own efforts. We may not be in the same straits, but our work should be as diligent. We do not need to use our work as an outlet for our neuroses (i.e., become "workaholics"). Ruth did not, in spite of a situation that might have made such conduct excusable.

In company with Ruth, Howard Ruff, and many, many others we all, at one time or another, experience the trials and setbacks of life. There are times during our earthly pilgrimage when we seem to be at our wit's end. Antoinette Wilson knew the experience well. She wrote to encourage us and give us hope:

> Are you standing at "Wit's End Corner,"
> Christian, with troubled brow?
> Are you thinking of what is before you,
> And all you are bearing now?
> Does all the world seem against you,
> And you in the battle alone?
> Remember—at "Wit's End Corner"
> Is just where God's power is shown.
>
> Are you standing at "Wit's End Corner,"
> Blinded with wearying pain,
> Feeling you cannot endure it,
> You cannot bear the strain,
> Bruised through the constant buffeting,
> Dizzy, and dazed, and numb?
> Remember—at "Wit's End Corner"
> Is where Jesus loves to come.
>
> Are you standing at "Wit's End Corner"?
> Your work before you spread,
> All lying begun, unfinished,
> And pressing on heart and head,
> Longing for strength to do it,
> Stretching out trembling hands?
> Remember—at "Wit's End Corner"
> The Burden-bearer stands.

Are you standing at "Wit's End Corner"?
Then you're just in the very spot
To learn the wondrous resources
Of Him who faileth not;
No doubt to a brighter pathway
Your footsteps will soon be moved,
But only at "Wit's End Corner"
Is the "God who is able" proved.[29]

How we overcome the vicissitudes of life depends on two things: (1) the way we think of ourselves,[30] and (2) our confidence in the Lord. Ruth illustrates for us the personal dynamics that will help us rise up from the ashes of our experience and persevere. She also shows us how God graciously works behind the scenes to accomplish His purpose for us. Although we may not be aware of His involvement, His guidance of us is as sure as His direction of Ruth's footsteps to the portion of the field that belonged to Boaz. We may therefore trust Him to work both in us and in our circumstances. In time He will lead our footsteps to "a brighter pathway."

4

THE DYNAMICS OF THE HELPING RELATIONSHIP

(Ruth 2:8-17)

Charles R. Swindoll is internationally known for his ability to expound the Scriptures with insight and understanding. In a recent message, he told of a television program he had watched. It concerned that most staid of subjects—a library. This program, however, was on our nation's Library of Congress. Swindoll told the following story:

> The program had all the markings of a slow-moving, dull documentary.
>
> About halfway through, Dr. Daniel Boorstin, our librarian of Congress, brought out a little box from a small closet that once held the library's rarities. The label on the box read: CONTENTS OF THE PRESIDENT'S POCKETS ON THE NIGHT OF APRIL 14, 1865.
>
> Since that was the fateful night Abraham Lincoln was assassinated, every viewer's attention was seized.
>
> Boorstin then proceeded to remove the items in the small container and display them on camera. There were five things in the box:
> - a handkerchief embroidered "A. Lincoln"
> - a country boy's pen knife
> - a spectacles case repaired with string
> - a purse containing a $5 bill—Confederate money
> - some old and worn newspaper clippings.
>
> "The clippings," said Boorstin, "were concerned with the great deeds of Abraham Lincoln. And one of them actually reports a speech by John Bright

which says that Abraham Lincoln is one of the greatest men of all times."

Today, that's common knowledge. The world now knows that British statesman John Bright was right in his assessment of Lincoln, but in 1865 millions shared quite a contrary opinion. The President's critics were fierce and many. His was a lonely agony that reflected the suffering and turmoil of a country ripped to shreds by hatred and a cruel, costly war.

There is something touchingly pathetic in the mental picture of this great leader seeking solace and self-assurance from the comfort of a few old newspaper clippings as he reads them under the flickering flame of a candle all alone in the Oval office.[1]

All of this brings us to consider the importance of encouragement and the way in which we can best use a unique gift of the Spirit that we all share—the gift of helps.

BIBLICAL EXAMPLES

There are two people in Scripture who illustrate clearly the gift of helps: Boaz and Barnabas.

Barnabas's real name was Joseph.[2] He was given the nickname *bar Nabas,* "son of consolation" or "son of encouragement" (Acts 4:36) because he was always helping people. He ministered to believers in the church in Jerusalem during times of persecution. As with his Master before him, he went about doing good. He helped the afflicted, comforted the distressed, and encouraged the downhearted. He even braved the censure of those in Jerusalem by introducing Paul, the recently converted persecutor of Christians, to the leaders of the church.

The other prominent person who illustrates the gift of helps is Boaz. His name, in all probability, means "in Him is strength." He was a kinsman of Naomi's late husband, Elimelech (2:1), but apparently the relationship was not close enough for him to be linked with Bethlehem's aristocracy.[3] He is referred to as an *'îš gibbōr hayil,* "a mighty man of valor." He was undoubtedly brave and resourceful—the kind of person the people of Bethlehem were glad to have as the leader of their little militia. Such a man was needed to protect their crops and herds from the Bedouin or Canaanites who would plunder them and carry off their few possessions.

When Boaz came down from the city to the field where his reapers were harvesting barley, he greeted them sincerely. He was not so occupied with his personal interests that he overlooked those poor who had come to glean in his field. As Watson has observed, "From the moment he appears in the narrative we note in him a certain largeness of character." And he is right. In Boaz piety, kindness, generosity, and empathy are finely blended. It is no wonder, therefore, that from the events of this chapter we learn the *how* as well as the *what* of the helping relationship.

PAST, PRESENT, AND PERSONAL

As we take up the story we see Boaz's kindly interest in a stranger who was gleaning in his field.

> And Boaz said to Ruth, "Do you not hear, my daughter?[5] Do not go to glean in another field, and also[6] do not leave this [one]; and you shall stay[7] with my young women. Your eyes[8] [shall be] on the field which they shall reap,[9] and you shall go after them;[10] have I not ordered the young men not to touch you.[11] When you [are] thirsty, then you shall go to the vessels and shall drink[12] from that which the young men draw." [2:8-9]

Boaz apparently was impressed with the report of his young overseer. He observed how diligently Ruth picked up the ears of grain that had fallen to the ground. He was filled with admiration for her, knowing that she was working hard to be able to support Naomi. He called her to him and, in words of positive assurance, impressed upon her that she was welcome to glean in his field. In fact, he went a step further and kindly insisted that she not go to any other field. Then, realizing that Ruth could not distinguish one field from another, he encouraged her to keep close to his maids.

Up to this point, nothing had been done by anyone in Bethlehem to make Ruth feel accepted. It is probable that as a foreigner she had been subjected to proud and scornful looks and a "We'll-wait-and-see-how-she-turns-out" attitude. In time, Ruth would win the hearts of everyone in the village, but until now she had had to struggle along on her own.

But why was Boaz so kind to Ruth?

Watson remarks, "The truth was that Ruth had met with a man of character who valued character."

Notice too the wisdom of Boaz. He made Ruth feel accepted: "You shall stay with my young women."

He was also considerate of her well-being: "I have ordered the young men not to touch you."

Finally, he facilitated the work she was doing by maximizing her time: "When you are thirsty [instead of going all the way back to Bethlehem] drink from the water my young men have drawn."

In these few verses we have important keys to the helping relationship.

ACCENTUATING THE POSITIVE

Boaz could easily have been patronizing, but he was not. He was wise enough to be helpful without robbing Ruth of the right to work (something our welfare agencies would do well to learn!).

In doing so he did not deprive her of the dignity of honest toil. He did assure her of her acceptance in his field.

Often in our desire to help others we try to do everything for them. We make them feel dependent upon us. When this happens, we erode their sense of esteem—that God-given right to derive satisfaction from honest labor. Then they begin to feel inferior. Resentment may develop, and with resentment there is experienced a latent hostility. Later on, we are surprised when those whom we have helped the most turn on us and castigate us. To use the old cliché, they "bite the hand that feeds them." Why? We did the right thing in the wrong way.

FEELING OF ISOLATION

Second, Boaz removed any feeling of isolation by encouraging Ruth to stay close to his young women. That gave her a sense of acceptance, of belonging.

It is that same feeling of acceptance and belongingness that people who need our help desire. Their lives have been disrupted. Others seem not to care or to be preoccupied with their own concerns. What they need is a genuine feeling of "I believe in you," "I approve of you," "I'm not afraid to be identified with you."

BASIC ISSUES

Third, Boaz was considerate of Ruth's well-being. He was aware of certain habit patterns and knew how easily his laborers might take advantage of a foreigner. He therefore took precautions to ensure Ruth's safety. Boaz knew how easy it would be for Ruth—poor and from Moab—to be looked upon as having no rights in Judah, so he instructed the young men not to harass or molest her.

Boaz was also considerate of Ruth's well-being while "on the job." He knew from experience how thirsty a person becomes working in the open field under the heat of the summer sun. To have to walk all the way to Bethlehem, draw water to quench one's thirst, and then return to the field would waste a considerable amount of time. To facilitate Ruth's gathering up of the grain, Boaz helped her maximize her time by giving her permission to drink from the water drawn by the young men.

The importance of these acts in the helping relationship cannot be overstressed. Our friendly guidance, timely precaution, and thoughtful consideration can make a person feel accepted, valued, and competent. Without them, our best efforts on behalf of others will tarnish before our eyes.

Fading Stigma

Ruth's response to such a kindly, considerate attitude on the part of Boaz was one of gratitude. She felt overwhelmed, and quickly sank to her knees. Then she touched her forehead to the ground before him.

> And she fell on her face, and bowed herself[13] to the earth, and said to him, "Why have I found favor in your eyes, that you should notice me, and I a stranger?"[14] And Boaz said to her, "All that you have done for [lit., with] your mother-in-law after the death of your husband, has been fully[15] told me; and how you forsook your father, and your mother, and the land of your birth, and came to a people whom you had not known before.[16] May *Yahweh* repay your work,[17] and may your wages [be] complete from *Yahweh*, the God of Israel, under whose wings[18] you have come to take refuge." And Ruth said, "May I continue to find favor in your eyes,[19] my lord, because you have spoken to the heart of [i.e., have cheered] your handmaid, though I am not as one of your handmaids."[20] [2:10-13]

Ruth was deeply touched by Boaz's magnanimity. She had not presumed on his kindness. She had set out that morning intent on gleaning sufficient grain for herself and Naomi. Now, she had been shown remarkable benevolence by a man she had only just met. Ruth knew nothing of Boaz's relationship to her late father-in-law. She was curious, however, and inquired of him the reason for the favor he had shown her.

Boaz replied that he had been told all that she had done for Naomi since Mahlon died. He was also aware that, as with Abraham before her, she had left her home and family and country for a land heretofore unknown to her. He also prayed that *Yahweh* would recompense her fully. Here was the encouragement she needed. Here too was the promise of hope for the future. As Morris has said, "[These words] represent the first cheerful thing recorded as happening to her since the death of her husband."[21] How easy they were to utter—and how necessary!

In Ruth's grateful response she placed herself below even those of Boaz's household who did the most menial work. In that we see her true humility.

In the words that pass between Boaz and Ruth we observe the kindness of Boaz matched by the graciousness of Ruth. He was prosperous, but he had not allowed his good fortune to cause him to forget the poor. She had been reduced to poverty but had not permitted such a reversal of fortune to make her hard and cynical.

In this respect, G. Campbell Morgan was right when he pointed out that the lives of Boaz and Ruth illustrate saintship. Ruth flourished amid circumstances calculated to discourage her. Boaz lived amid people of privilege in times of degeneracy, yet he did not permit the social mores of his day to squeeze him into their mold. Both Ruth and Boaz had a unique trust in the Lord. They prove: (1) that outward circumstances neither make nor mar the children of God, (2) that faith is still the key to appropriating the blessings of God, and (3) that by our obedience to the revealed will of God, He makes us part of a plan that exceeds our ability to imagine.[22]

RURAL HOSPITALITY

Boaz had already made Ruth feel accepted, valued, and able. In a word, he had encouraged her. Now he would introduce her to the circle of his workers. He desired that they receive her with typical rural hospitality.

> And Boaz said to Ruth at mealtime,[23] "Come here, and you shall eat of the bread and dip your morsel in the vinegar."[24] And she sat at the side of the harvesters. And Boaz served[25] her roasted grain,[26] and she ate and was satisfied and had some left over.[27] When she arose to glean, Boaz commanded his young men, saying, "She may glean[28] even among the sheaves, and [do not do anything that would] shame her.[29] And also you shall purposely pull out for her [some grain] from the bundles and shall leave it; and she shall glean and you shall not rebuke her." So Ruth gleaned in the field until evening. Then she beat out what she had gleaned, and it was about an ephah of barley. [2:14-17]

The scene described in these verses has been observed by travelers in the Middle East. Edward Robinson tells of what he saw while on a visit to the Holy Land.

> In one field, as we approached Kubeibeh, nearly 200 reapers and gleaners were at work; the latter being nearly as numerous as the former. A few were taking their refreshment, and offered us some of their "parched corn." In the season of harvest the grains of wheat, not yet fully dry and hard, are roasted in a pan or on an iron plate, and constitute a very palatable article of food. This is eaten with bread, or instead of it. Indeed, the use of it is so common at this time among the labouring classes, that this parched wheat is sold in markets. . . . The whole scene of the reapers and gleaners, and their "parched corn," gave us a lively representation of the story of Ruth and ancient harvest-time in the fields of Boaz.[30]

It is interesting to notice that Boaz ate *with* his servants. He did not feel the need to keep them at a distance. Men of character do not need to enforce respect. They have earned it because of *what* (not who) they are. They need no artificial hierarchy, titles, or tokens of superiority. They are assured and confident. Such men do not require the homage of those of lower social status.

It is also interesting to note the ease and sense of assurance that characterized Ruth. She had only recently told Boaz that she was not even to be numbered among his *šiphâh,* or "maidservants," a more menial designation even than *ʾamâh,* "handmaid." Yet when invited to join him for the noonday meal, she was able to do so without any false modesty or embarrassment.

Boaz performed the duty of a host by serving Ruth. In that we see more of his special kindness. Such action would be marked by his servants, and out of respect for so kind an employer they would be more inclined to treat Ruth the same way.

The fact that Boaz gave Ruth more food than she needed was also indicative of Boaz's special favor. It calls to mind Joseph, as prime minister of Egypt, entertaining his brothers and giving Benjamin five times as much as any of the others (Gen. 43:34).

Furthermore, Boaz instructed his servants to allow Ruth to glean between the standing sheaves and also told them purposely to drop small bundles for her to pick up as she worked along behind them. He was concerned that Ruth's efforts on behalf of Naomi be amply rewarded.

Boaz's servants cooperated so well that by evening Ruth had to beat out what she had gathered before she could take it home. While it is difficult to know exactly how much an ephah was, authorities claim that it was about thirty pounds.

A HELPING HAND

All of this brings us to consider the essence of the helping relationship—*encouragement,* the kind of encouragement that meets a person's physiological and psychological needs. Ruth's physiological needs were basic: food, shelter, and clothing. Hunger was a real threat to both her and her mother-in-law. Ruth's psychological needs were likewise basic. She needed to feel accepted, valued, and capable.

BRUISED EXPECTATIONS

One of our most basic needs is for a sense of acceptance or belonging. When all is going well, we tend to take the blessings of life for granted. We are content if we can keep our trials under control. When adversity strikes, however, our friends frequently desert us. They have enough problems of their own without taking on any of ours (unlike Gal. 6:2). At a time like that we are tempted to feel we do not belong, that nobody wants us, and that we are all alone.

The exercise of the gift of helps begins with an acceptance of the person. This is a rare quality today, for all of us feel depersonalized. To the IRS we are a computer number; to the state or federal government we are a statistic; and to charitable organizations we represent a financial contribution. We all need to feel wanted, to be accepted, to be a part of the community, and never is this more true than when we are hurting. Those who wish to be used of God to lift up the downcast and heal broken hearts must, therefore, begin with the acceptance of the individual. Such an attitude is of great encouragement to those who are experiencing the inequities or capricious reverses of life.

UNCERTAIN FUTURE

Second, there is the matter of personal worth. Anxieties over one's safety or questions whether life holds promise of anything better may reduce a person's effectiveness. This in turn may hinder him from getting back on his feet.

Boaz knew the risks associated with the harvest and took immediate steps to ensure Ruth's personal safety. To him she was a person of worth, not the member of a despised race. That done, Ruth could put forth her best effort.

This sense of being valued by another, of having worth (or significance) for who we are rather than for the work we do, is sorely needed in commerce and industry, education and politics, church and society. Without it we feel depersonalized; with it we feel accepted and assured. All too often in our homes and businesses people are treated like things, and things are invested with worth as if they were people. Such a breakdown in the interpersonal process leads to the establishment of "adversary" relationships in which workers do as little for their employers as possible, and employers feel they must exert pressure on their employees to get them to work at even marginal levels of efficiency.

How beautifully Boaz illustrates for us the difference respect for the person makes in one's attitude. And through his conduct, others imbibed his outlook.

TIMELY ASSISTANCE

Third, there is the important matter of helping needy persons maximize their own efforts.

I recall my mother describing some timely help given her by her pastor's wife. My mother and brother were moving into a new house, in which the previous owners had kept a maid to cook and clean. The house was immaculate; the kitchen was a mess.

On the day my mother moved in she found, so she said, "Ten years of dust, pieces of stale bread, hardened spaghetti, and old pop bottle tops against the wall where the refrigerator had stood." (Her pastor's wife concurred, saying it was the filthiest kitchen she had ever seen.) The stove and oven carried an accumulation of grime and grease that had not been removed since their installation.

All the joy of moving into a new house was gone. Cleaning the kitchen had taken on "Himalayan" proportions. Just then the doorbell rang. The movers had arrived with all the furniture and at least 132 boxes of assorted shapes and sizes.

To the credit of the pastor's wife, she tackled the kitchen, sweeping away a decade of accumulated dust and garbage, cleaning unbelievable grime from the stove and oven, and scrubbing the floor. That one room alone took an entire day to clean.

The result? My mother could maximize her time and energies showing the movers where the furniture should go and then unpacking and putting into closets the contents of the boxes.

Only my mother really knew how encouraging it was to have such timely help.

No Longer Hopeless

The ministry of helping others is essentially a ministry of encouragement. Ruth acknowledged this. She said to Boaz, "You have spoken to the heart of your maidservant" (2:13). His words and attitudes had heartened her.

The steps that Boaz took, and which we who wish to use this gift of the Holy Spirit must take, include:
- accepting the individual as he is, and making him feel that he belongs
- treating him as a person of worth and insuring that his rights are respected
- assisting him to obtain the best results from his time and resources.

Such a ministry of encouragement is open to each of us. Jonathan engaged in it when he sought out David at Horesh and "strengthened his hands in God" (1 Sam. 23:15-18). He emboldened his friend to look away from himself to the One who is a very present Helper of those who are in trouble (Ps. 46:1).

The apostle Paul exhorted believers to be constantly encouraging one another and building one another up in the faith (1 Thess. 5:11). Isaiah spoke about encouraging those who are exhausted with life's conflicts and strengthening those who feel they cannot go on any more (Isa. 35:3). And

Paul, who knew how much we all need a lifting up of our spirits, spoke of the encouragement that comes to our hearts as we meditate on God's Word (Rom. 15:4).

Such encouragement will enable those who are cast down to enjoy a measure of happiness and contentment, regardless of their temporal circumstances.

5

GOD'S PROVISION FOR MAN'S NEED

(Ruth 2:18-23)

Certain words need no explanation: *Rolls Royce, NASA, patriotism, touchdown*. They are synonymous with quality of workmanship, space exploration, pride in one's country, and the discipline and teamwork that always precede achievement.

In his recent book *Six Great Ideas*, Mortimer Adler discusses certain other words: *truth, goodness*, and *beauty* (the standards by which we assess worth); *liberty, equality*, and *justice* (the principles that govern our actions). Adler says, "The words that name the great ideas are all of them words of ordinary, everyday speech. They do not belong to the private jargon of a specialized branch of knowledge."[1] However, the very fact that Adler has found it necessary to write an entire book about these words indicates how little we understand their real meaning.

There are other words that also need explaining, for our perceptions about them are hazy and ill-defined. These words include *character, wealth, happiness*, and *devotion*.

We found in chapter 4 that the two great tests of character are wealth and poverty. In the case of Boaz we learned that a true test of character is the way a person treats those who can do nothing for him. In the next chapter we will observe that another test of character is not what a person does in the light when his actions are in plain view, but what he does in the dark, when no one is watching.

We too often equate having money with being happy. We have been reared to believe that the Constitution guarantees us the right to "life, liberty, and the [purchase] of happiness." Few realize, however, that riches do not bring happiness.

Howard Hughes died in April 1976. He had amassed a fortune estimated at two billion dollars. Shortly before becoming a recluse, the industrialist—aviator—film-maker was interviewed by a reporter. The conversation was taped and played on NBC News the night Hughes died. One of the questions asked the billionaire was if his wealth and power had brought him any lasting happiness.

"No," replied Hughes, "I would not say that I am a happy man!"[2]

Happiness is not to be found in the abundance of our possessions or even in doing what we like, but in an inner contentment and in enjoying what we have to do. True happiness is more a matter of personality than surroundings. It is found in the contentment that fills the soul even in the midst of the most distressing circumstances. That is why one sage remarked, "If you can't find contentment in yourself, it is useless to seek for it elsewhere."

And then there is devotion—the dedication of one's entire being to a person or a cause. Ruth's devotion was to her mother-in-law. She did not regard the care of Naomi a distasteful chore to be performed with reluctance and bragged about afterwards in the village. Consequently, the happiness she enjoyed came through the glad performance of the duty she had willingly undertaken.

BEYOND THE VISIBLE

Whereas our story thus far has been concerned with the plight of two widows and the commanding presence of Boaz, we shall miss the whole point of this short book if we neglect to see God's hand at work behind the scenes. In the law He had pledged Himself to be the Defender and Sustainer of widows and orphans. He called Himself their Helper and Supporter (Pss. 68:5-6a; 146:9). He promised to visit retribution and the severest of penalties upon those who defrauded and oppressed them (Ps. 94:6-11; Ezek. 22:7; Mal. 3:5).[3]

As He cared for the needs of widows and orphans, however, God chose to use means. The people of Israel were to be His instruments in providing for them (Deut. 14:29), and the leaders were to be responsible for defending them (Isa. 1:17, 23). In Ruth, Boaz is one through whom the Lord works to alleviate Naomi's and Ruth's privation (cf. Gal. 6:10).

BREAD-AND-BUTTER ISSUES

Chapter 5 concluded with Ruth beating out the barley she had gleaned. As we take up the narrative once more, she had returned to the village and shown Naomi what she had.

> And Ruth gleaned in the field until evening and beat out what she had gleaned, and it was about an ephah of barley.[4] And she took it up and went to the city. And her mother-in-law saw[5] what she had gleaned; and Ruth [also] brought out and gave to Naomi what remained [of the parched corn and vinegar] after she had eaten her fill.[6] [2:17-18]

The scene is not too difficult to imagine. Ruth had worked hard all day. With a sense of satisfaction she had beat out the grain into a shawl and carried it up the path to the city. We do not know who saw her as she entered Bethlehem hot and tired from her exertion and walked down the lanes that led to Naomi's humble cottage.

Naomi too had spent a busy day. She had completed whatever cleaning remained to be done, obtained some straw for bedding, and now waited for Ruth to return. She had probably heard some of the other harvesters as they walked down the street, and it would have been natural for her to feel anxious over Ruth. Where was she? Why had she not come? Had something happened to her?

At last Naomi heard Ruth approaching. Hardly knowing what to expect, she opened the door to let her in. As Ruth stepped in with her shawl filled with barley she made her way to the rough-hewn table in the center of the room. Her burden was a heavy one. She then opened her shawl and showed Naomi what she had gleaned. The text also tells us that Ruth gave to her mother-in-law some of the food Boaz had given her during the noon meal.

Evidence of Ruth's earlier hunger may be found in the fact that she had eaten her fill of the food Boaz served to her. The text does not tell us when she and Naomi had had their last meal, and the exertion of the morning may well have sapped her strength. There is also a subtle indication in the text that Naomi likewise was ravenous. Without being disrespectful, one gains the impression from Naomi's conversations (see 1:8-9, 11-13; 2:19) that she was an exuberant kind of woman. She appears to have been effervescent and talkative—the kind of person you love having in the house because she is always in good spirits. The text, however, does not contain any word of surprise from Naomi until *after* she had eaten Ruth's "leftovers."

The *New American Standard Bible* (perhaps our most accurate version) translates verse 19*a* as follows: "Her mother-in-law *then* said to her, 'Where did you glean today and where did you work?' May he who took notice of you be blessed'" (italics added).[8]

If our sensitivity to the subtleties of the text has led us to the right conclusion, then we may say that it was only after Naomi's hunger had been satisfied and her spirits had revived that her curiosity asserted itself. Her question, "Where did you glean today and where did you work?" is an example of Hebrew poetry in the form of parallelism. That in itself is indicative of an exuberant spirit. Under normal circumstances Naomi was evidently a person who loved life and whose cheerful disposition caused people to like her. And when that is added to her obvious interest in and concern for other people it is not hard to see why she endeared herself to her daughter-in-law.

All of this is underscored by Naomi's next remark, "May he be blessed who took notice of you." The verb *bārak,* "to bless," occurs about 330 times in the Bible. It is first used of God blessing Adam and Eve (cf. Gen. 1:22, 28; see also 9:1; 12:2-3). It represents the essence of goodness and stands in stark contrast to paganism where power resides in the ability to curse (or bring evil upon) another.

The very fact that Naomi invoked happiness upon their unnamed benefactor showed her basic disposition. It was characterized by godliness and an absence of selfishness. Cox writes:

> We are made to feel that we are with those in whom piety is an active and ruling power. Any woman, however selfish or godless, might have been as surprised and glad as Naomi was at this unexpected turn of fortune. But she, before even her question can be answered, and moved simply by the manifest happiness of Ruth in the abundance of her gleanings, "blesses" the man who has given her this happiness. For this she does not need to know who he is.[9]

SHARED VALUES

Ruth too revealed a guileless spirit: We read, "And she told her mother-in-law with whom she had worked, and she said, 'The name of the man with whom I worked today[10] [is] Boaz'" (2:19*b*).

Ruth's response to Naomi's questions was clear and direct. She was quite unaware that Boaz was a relative of her late father-in-law, she had not the slightest intimation of the role Boaz would play in her future. Furthermore, the innocent way in which she mentioned Boaz's name shows that she had no idea of the dramatic import of her words. As Edward Campbell has pointed out, "The audience [listening to the story of Ruth gleaning in the field of Boaz] has known all along, but the dramatic suspense lies with the recognition that Naomi has not."[11] To her the name of Boaz comes as a complete surprise.

With the mention of Boaz's name Naomi apparently began to see the Lord's hand in the affairs of the day. "She exclaimed, 'Blessed be he of *Yahweh* who has not forsaken His kindness with the living[12] and with the dead.' And Naomi [again] said to Ruth, 'The man [is] near [of kin] to us; he [is] one of our redeemers'" (2:20).

It would seem that at once Naomi grasped the significance of her young relative's kindness. She may have experienced one of those situations in life when a person senses something intuitively ahead of the ability to express it. In any event, she broke out into praise once more.

Naomi's words, however, pose an interpretative problem for us. She first gave thanks for Boaz, "Blessed be he of *Yahweh*," and with a deep sense of gratitude recognized his kindness to her and Ruth. She then went on to say, "who has not forsaken his kindness. . ." and at first we are inclined to take the *who* as referring to Boaz. Morris, however, alerts us that "the whole drift of the passage shows that Naomi is thinking of God (cf. Gen. 24:27)."[13] This being the case, it underscores Naomi's recognition of God's grace. *He* has not forsaken them or their family.

Cox summarizes Naomi's experience for us.

> If we would enter into the force of this outburst of praise, we must remember that Naomi had lost her faith—not in God, indeed, but in the good will of God for her. She had thought that He was turned to be her foe, and the foe of the husband and sons who had been snatched from her by a premature death. They were dead because they had sinned in forsaking the land of the Covenant. She was bereaved, forsaken, "empty," because she had shared their sin. So, at least, she had conceived. But now, in the wonderful Providence which had led Ruth to find a friend in her valiant and wealthy kinsman, she [sees] proof that God had not wholly abandoned her, that He had not left off His kindness whether to her or to the beloved dead. No one who has witnessed such a [reversion] from spiritual despair to renewed hope in the Divine goodness and compassion will marvel at the ecstasy which breathes in Naomi's words. Rather, he will be sure that it would be long before she could recover her composure, and listen to what Ruth had still to tell; he will feel that in this brief exclamation of praise we have, compressed into a single sentence, the substance of many heartfelt thanksgivings.[14]

SEED THOUGHTS

Ruth's nonchalant mention of Boaz's name had sparked Naomi's thought processes. Could her daughter-in-law's chance meeting with Boaz be the prelude to a long-term solution to their problem? The abundance of barley that Ruth had brought home might indicate his initial interest in her. There were problems, however, that stood in the way of

Boaz's exercise of the right of redemption, and so Naomi contented herself with saying to Ruth, "The man [is] near [of kin] to us; he [is] one of our *gō'elim* (redeemers)."

The word *gō'ēl*, "redeemer," needs some explanation.[15] A *gō'ēl* was a member of the family—sometimes a father, but more often a brother—to whom fell the duty of "redeeming" property (Lev. 25:23-28)[16] or persons (Lev. 25:47-55),[17] or of executing "blood vengeance"—the redressing of a wrong done a member of the family (Num. 35:12, 19, 21, 24, 27; Deut. 19:6, 12; Josh. 20:3, 5, 9).[18] As a relative of Elimelech's, Boaz was one of their redeemers.

Associated with the duties of a redeemer was levirate marriage. In 1:11-13 Naomi had made reference to this ancient Hebrew custom.[19] The custom existed among the Hebrews *before* the giving of the law (cf. Gen. 38:8) and involved the marriage of a man to his deceased brother's widow (in the event his brother died childless). Later on, the custom was given the sanction of Mosaic legislation (Deut. 25:5-10). For a brother to care for his sister-in-law and raise up a child to bear the name of the deceased and inherit his estate was regarded as *an act of love!*

Because Boaz was related to Elimelech, Naomi referred to him as "one of our close relatives"—one who might perform the duty of *gō'ēl*. It seems as if the wheels of her mind were already turning, and she was hopeful that he would exercise the right of redemption on their behalf.[20] But because Naomi was beyond child-bearing age, perhaps Boaz may be prepared to marry Ruth instead. Such a marriage would be unprecedented in the history of her people. It would necessitate that Boaz act in the *spirit* of the law rather than adhere to its letter.

TIMELY COUNSEL

Naomi, however, did not become so preoccupied with her plans that she failed to listen to what Ruth was saying. This is a common problem and results in the breakdown of communication within many homes. Naomi listened to all that Ruth had to say. She picked up on a small item that Ruth had "dropped" in her recounting of the day's events, and that became the basis of her heartfelt counsel. We read it in verses 21 and 22:

> And Ruth the Moabitess[21] said, "And he surely said to me, 'You shall stay close by the young men[22] whom I have [i.e. who work for me] until they have completed the whole harvest which I have [i.e. all my fields, both barley and wheat].'"

> And Naomi said to Ruth, her daughter-in-law, "[It is] good, my daughter, that you go out with his young women, so that [men] will not attack[23] you in another field."

The situation described in these verses is not difficult to understand. Naomi was concerned for Ruth's safety. She was fearful lest someone take advantage of her, and therefore stressed the importance of Ruth's remaining close to Boaz's young women.

Ruth was certainly teachable. She also listened to all Naomi had to say. The inspired writer concludes this portion of his account with the following summary: "And Ruth stayed close to Boaz's young women until the completion of the barley harvest and the wheat harvest[24]; and she lived with her mother-in-law" (2:23).

FOOD FOR THOUGHT

As we review these verses we learn several important lessons:
- the tensions of life should in no way lessen the satisfaction we receive from doing our appointed task
- the encouragement we receive from the Lord should reinforce our commitment to Him and His will for us
- in all things we should exhibit a teachable spirit.

THE MATTER OF TENSION

The "Royal Preacher" of Ecclesiastes spent time considering the plight of man on the earth (i.e. "under the sun"). He concluded that because of all the vexations and inequities of life and man's common end (the grave), "There is nothing better for a man than that he should make his soul enjoy the good of his labor." Then he added, "This also I saw, that it was from the hand of God" (Eccles. 2:24).

We are often caught up in tensions that rob us of our peace and deprive us of our happiness. We are subject to exploitation by others, endure unwarranted criticism, and face the pressures of competition from our colleagues. Solomon recommended that his readers develop a spirit of contentment that would ease those tensions: "Better a handful [of bread] with quietness, than both hands full with travail and vexation of spirit" (Eccles. 4:6). His counsel was aimed at reducing stress and enabling those who would heed his advice to live happier, more contented lives.

It should be admitted that for some people a certain amount of tension leads to productivity. They are reactive by nature, generally leave things to the last minute, and work best under pressure. They are not easy to live with or work for, and their personality bent deprives them of much of the happiness they could otherwise enjoy.

Others are caught up on the treadmill of more money and more possessions. The pressure they feel to produce more, acquire more, and hoard more develops tensions that result in high blood pressure, sleeplessness, irritability, poor interpersonal relations, and a variety of physiological problems.

The evident ability of Ruth to cope with the pressure of providing for herself and Naomi, and Naomi's evident ability to exhibit gratitude and enjoy Ruth's company, model for us the way they overcame the tensions that would naturally be caused by their situation.

The antidote to worry is trust. Naomi had only recently returned to the place of blessing. Her trust was in the Lord. He assured her of His favor by blessing Ruth's efforts, and out of a heart filled with gratitude she praised Him for His goodness to her (2:20).

THIS THING CALLED CONFIDENCE

The tangible evidence of God's love and favor toward her and Ruth gave Naomi confidence as they faced the future together. Their problems remained. They were still penniless, but Naomi's former despondency (cf. 1:11-14, 20-21) had now turned to a glad assurance. She therefore praised God that He had not forsaken His *ḥesed* ("lovingkindness") to her or her husband.

Confidence in the biblical sense is more than a PMA—a positive mental attitude. It comes from a heart that is right with God, observes evidences of His reinforcement of faith and trust, and therefore gladly commits to Him its tomorrows.

These evidences of God's grace toward us may come from a variety of sources: His Word, circumstances, or through a friend.

Some years ago I was visiting in a city. A friend of mine asked if I would visit one of his parishioners who was in the hospital awaiting surgery for the fusing of two vertebrae of her spine. Her husband had recently deserted her, and she felt very alone in the world. In addition, all my friends' efforts had failed to lift her spirits.

When I entered that hospital room and introduced myself, I did not find a woman in need of counsel or encouragement. She had been reading the book of Psalms and had been led by David's example to place herself and her tomorrows entirely in God's hands. That included the outcome of the surgery the next day and the three full months of convalescence that would follow. Her appropriation of the encouragement offered her in the Word of God was sufficient to sustain her.

There are also times when God uses circumstances to encourage us. These may be the result of prayer or connected with the more mundane things of life—like having our car start when it is −20° outside, when schedules can be adjusted to meet our needs, or when a "chance" encounter results in the solution of a dilemma we happened to be facing. When those things happen, we should see God's hand behind the temporal circumstance and be appropriately thankful.

When it comes to the way *we* can bring encouragement to others, we should never forget that the Lord may have placed us in that situation to be His "agent" through whom help or blessing may be brought to a needy soul.

Cox expressed it this way:

> When we consider how potent our kindness may be in quickening the sense of God's kindness and compassion in a neighbour's heart, and how potent, therefore, our lack of kindness and compassion may be, in inducing or confirming a neighbour's despair, we may well tremble at the responsibility which, at any moment, may fall on us. It was not till Naomi arrived in Bethlehem, and saw her neighbours indifferent and apathetic, however curious and inquisitive they were, that she concluded herself to be shut out from the mercy of God. It was only when Boaz showed a little kindness to her daughter—such a kindness as we may show a neighbour any day—that she felt the door of mercy was once more thrown open to her.[25]

This truth places a solemn responsibility on each one of us.

TEACHABLE SPIRIT

Third, there is also the importance of a teachable spirit. It is interesting to notice over and over again Ruth's willing subordination of herself to her mother-in-law. She heeded Naomi's counsel and never complained about her advice. And in the next chapter we will have a further illustration of Ruth's teachable spirit.

Being teachable is indispensable to our personal growth. Those who "know everything" and cannot be taught anything demonstrate by that attitude their immaturity and resistence to growth.

The truth did not threaten Ruth, and she gladly accepted the counsel given her (cf. 2:8-9, 22). As a new convert, Ruth was learning about the customs and the culture of God's people. She did not expect a utopian ideal and took seriously Naomi's warning that she might be sexually molested if she went to some other field.

We see Ruth's maturity in her attitude. She was not a wide-eyed "Pollyanna" believing that now she had come to trust "under *Yahweh's* wings" (2:12) everything would be perfect. Furthermore, she did not regard Naomi's warning as needless and reply, "Don't worry, Mom; I know how to look after myself." Instead, she accepted Naomi's words in the spirit in which they were given and incorporated all that she had seen and heard as a part of the growth experiences of life.

From Ruth's example we learn that through our teachableness in little things we prepare ourselves (as Ruth did) for the momentous experiences of life. Those experiences only come when we are prepared for them.

6

MOVED BY LOVE

(Ruth 3:1-13)

How would you describe *love*?

Imagine that you are on a television game show and have been asked to write down your view of love in twenty-five words or less. What would you say?

When pushed for some profound insights into the nature of love, certain celebrities said:

- "Love is the fairest flower that blooms in God's garden."
- "Love is a ticklish sensation around the heart that can't be scratched."
- "Love is like a vaccination. When it takes hold you don't have to be told."
- "Of all human passions love is the strongest, for it attacks simultaneously the head, the heart, and the senses."
- "Love makes a fellow feel funny and act stupid."

Now in all candor such verbiage does not aid our understanding of love!

To a Hollywood producer, love is a temporary relationship satisfying the urge of the moment, but the viewer is always aware that next week the encounter will be with someone else. To the fellow in the office with a wife and three children at home, love is often identified with a quiet weekend somewhere with his wife so that they can recapture the mystery of their early romance. Our view of love tends to reflect our individual personalities and express our own needs and desires. It is, therefore, often subjective.

Our lack of clarity about what constitutes real love has led some clinicians to try to objectively analyze it. After extensive research the famous psychiatrist Dr. Harry Stack Sullivan described love in the following cautious terms: "When a person's care and concern for another is as great as his care and concern for himself, then a state of love may be said to exist."[1]

That definition bears a close resemblance to Matthew 22:39. What it leaves out is the first prerequisite, the vertical dimension (expressed in verse 37, NASB: "You shall love the Lord your God . . . ") upon which the horizontal one depends, for love (to be sustaining) must be more than the measure of our concern for ourselves.

From a biblical point of view, love is seen in *the desire for the highest good in the one loved, even to the point of self-sacrifice*. Only a definition such as that can satisfy the demands of passages of Scripture like John 3:16 and 15:13.

UNCERTAIN FUTURE

As we examine chapter 3 of Ruth we find three illustrations of mature love. First, there is Naomi. Acting out of a heart filled with love for Ruth, she desired to see her happily married, comfortably ensconced in a home, and able to enjoy the blessings of a husband's companionship and protection. To accomplish that she devised a plan that, if successful, would see Ruth happily united to a noble man while she (Naomi) may have to endure a lonely, poverty-stricken old age.

The second illustration of mature love is Ruth. She was aware of Naomi's motives, and in carrying out her plan had every intention of ensuring Naomi's protection. Boaz realized this and praised her: "May you be blessed of *Yahweh,* my daughter. You have shown in this last kindness [to Naomi, in contracting a marriage within the family of Elimelech] to be better than the first [when you left your homeland in order to care for your mother-in-law] for you have not sought for marriage by going after the young man, whether poor or rich" (3:10).

Finally, Boaz illustrated his genuine love for the family of Elimelech by expressing his willingness to provide for both Naomi and Ruth (cf. 4:9-10). As Leggett has pointed out, "It is important to recognize that the levirate duty entailed a sacrifice of love." Then, commenting on Boaz's words in Ruth 4:10, he emphasizes the selflessness of the "redeemer" who, in perpetuating the "name of the dead in his inheritance," performed an act of love that never could be repaid.[2]

With these thoughts in mind let us observe the outworking of mature love in the relationships of Naomi, Ruth, and Boaz.

And Naomi, Ruth's mother-in-law, said to her, "My daughter, have I not been seeking[3] rest[4] for you, that it may be well with you? And now, is not Boaz of our kindred,[5] with whose young women you have been? Behold, he [is] winnowing barley [at] the threshing floor[6] tonight.[7] Now you shall wash and anoint yourself,[8] and put on your garments,[9] and go down[10] to the threshing floor; [but] do not let yourself be known to the man[11] until after he has finished eating and drinking. And it shall be, when he lies down that you shall know [i.e., take note of] the place where he lies down, and you shall go in and uncover his feet,[12] and lie down. And he will tell you what you are to do." And Ruth said to her, "All that you say, I will do." And she went down to the threshing floor and did according to all that her mother-in-law [had] commanded her. [3:1-6]

A RESPECTABLE HAVEN

Here is Naomi's deep concern for her daughter-in-law. She desired to see Ruth married. The text gives evidence that she had been giving considerable thought regarding how to accomplish that desire. As Naomi shared her plan with Ruth we become aware of her loving concern.

Naomi has been severely criticized for suggesting that Ruth go at night to the threshing floor outside Bethlehem and ask Boaz to marry her. Some commentators have become so defensive that they have overlooked the positive teaching of the passage. Naomi desired only what was best for Ruth. A widow's lot was a hard one, and her livelihood was precarious.[13] It would be many months before the next harvest. Naomi was anxious for her daughter-in-law's safety. She desired for Ruth that security and blessing, protection and companionship that can only stem from the union of a man and a woman.

Interestingly, Naomi again used the word *mānôah,* "rest," to describe that union. But the word implies more than a home. Inherent within it is the idea of mutual love and acceptance, a cessation from striving to attain something. It is used in some contexts of the complete envelopment or permeation of someone by something, which evokes a sense of peace or quietness—hence the use of the word "rest." It is this atmosphere of mutual love, respect, and security that Naomi wanted for Ruth, and marriage was the only such haven for a woman.

Since Ruth first mentioned Boaz's kindness to her (see 2:19), Naomi had time to watch Boaz. She had not seen him in more than a decade, and she wished to see if he would be a suitable husband for Ruth. Apparently what Naomi observed had impressed her. Boaz appeared to be one of those rare individuals who was motivated by principles, not expediency—he wanted to do what was right regardless of personal preference or convenience. Furthermore, he had given evidence of being one who could be trusted with the welfare of another. All of that commended him to Naomi.

Having checked everything carefully, Naomi now made her proposal to Ruth. Her words were full of kindness: "My daughter, have I not been seeking rest for you?" (3:1), which is a Hebraism stating a positive fact. Naomi was also reassuring. She reminded Ruth of Boaz's kindnesses to her and that she had spent the past six weeks with his maids. Her plan, however, was not without its difficulties. It would require prompt action, for (and this fact may have only recently come to her attention) Boaz would be threshing grain that night. It would also require courage, for Ruth would need to go to the threshing floor at night and there ask Boaz to marry her.

For Naomi's plan to succeed would require the "help of the Almighty" for, as Moshe Weinfeld has said, this natural story, "in which everything moves by human agents and, as it were, without divine interference, actually serves as a testimony for the wondrous ways in which God leads men [generically speaking] toward His destiny . . . . The occurrences which look like a chain of natural happenings evolving one from the other, reveal themselves in the end as the outcome of God's plan."[14]

Naomi was unaware of the Lord's hand in these matters, but she was satisfied that Boaz could be trusted with Ruth's safety. She therefore recommended that Ruth bathe and anoint herself with perfume, put on her clothes, and go down to the threshing floor. After Boaz had retired, she was to uncover his feet and lie down next to him. When he awoke, she would ask him to marry her.

Naomi was confident that Boaz and Ruth would conduct themselves with due circumspection. Morris has pointed out, "The fact that [Naomi] was prepared to urge this course on Ruth is the measure of her trust in both participants."[15] Another couple, less mature in themselves and less committed to doing what was right, might not be trusted in a similar situation.

But Naomi was also wise to caution Ruth. Immoral practices associated with fertility rites were practiced on pagan threshing floors. Ruth, therefore, would need to be careful as well as discreet, and "not make herself known" to Boaz until well after dark when everyone else was asleep.

THE LOCAL SETTING

Threshing floors in those times were frequently situated in the

immediate vicinity of the harvest field. A raised, level area was used, and
the floor was packed down hard to provide a durable surface. The grain
was placed in a pile on the floor and a heavy, flat slab of rock was
sometimes dragged over it by oxen.

When the grain had been separated from the stalk and chaff, it was
thrown into the air with a fork against a strong wind. The heavier grain
would fall to the ground, but the lighter stalk and chaff would be blown to
the end of the threshing floor where a slow fire would be burning (cf.
Matt. 3:12).

Evenings were normally chosen for this kind of work, perhaps because
then the wind blew more steadily from one direction. In any event, the
owner or foreman would usually sleep on the threshing floor with his men
to protect his harvest from robbers.

Those particulars will help us visualize the scene as Ruth followed with
precision the instructions of her mother-in-law.

> And Ruth went down to the grain floor and did according to all[16] that her
> mother-in-law had commanded her.[17] And Boaz ate and drank,[18] and his heart
> [felt] good;[19] and he went to lie down at the end of the heap [of grain].[20] And
> Ruth came in quietly[21] and uncovered his feet[22] and lay down. And it came to
> pass [lit., and it was], in the middle of the night,[23] that the man trembled[24] and
> turned himself, and, behold, a woman[25] [was] lying at his feet. And he said,
> "Who are you?"[26] And she said, "I [am] Ruth, your handmaid,[27] spread your
> wing[28] over your handmaid, for you [are] a redeemer."[29] And Boaz said,
> "Blessed[30] [be] you of *Yahweh,* my daughter, you have done well [in that] your
> kindness in the end [is] more than at the beginning,[31] and you have not gone
> after the young men,[32] either poor or rich. And now, my daughter,[33] do not fear;
> all that you say I will do for you, for all the gate[34] of my people knows that you
> are a woman of valor [i.e., worth].[35] And now, surely [it is] true that I [am] a
> redeemer,[36] but also there is a redeemer nearer than I.[37] Stay [here] tonight,[38]
> and it shall be in the morning, if he will redeem you, good; he will redeem
> [you];[39] and if he is not pleased[40] to redeem you, then, as *Yahweh* lives,[41] I will
> redeem you. Lie down until the morning." [3:6-13]

Those verses are worthy of extended treatment, for they are filled with
important lessons. We will take note of only a few of them.

CLIMAX OF THE HARVEST

Boaz and his men sat around the fire eating and drinking, and then lay
down on the floor for the night. Boaz took his place near the heap of grain
whereas his men probably chose places to rest at the end of the threshing
floor near the fire.

In the light of the flickering flame Ruth took note of where Boaz lay down. When everyone was asleep and the fire had died to little more than glowing embers, she crept quietly to the place where Boaz was sleeping and, uncovering his feet so that he would awaken when they become cold, she also lay down and waited.

IMPORTANT PRINCIPLES

Ruth's actions illustrate certain important biblical principles:
- that for the provision of God's Word to be fulfilled, the believer must first be completely identified with the Lord and His cause (see 1:16b; cf. Matt. 6:33)
- that the promises of God's Word must be claimed by faith

Ruth had met the first of those conditions when she turned her back on her home, her people, and her former manner of life, and in words of exquisite beauty forever identified herself with Naomi, Naomi's people, and Naomi's God (cf. 2:12).

Ruth went down to the threshing floor, claiming the fulfillment of the provisions of the covenant (cf. Deut. 25:5-10). Her faith may be seen in her belief in a possibility against all probabilities. Hers was not a faddish faith, for such can be as dangerous as faith that is false. Rather it was a faith that is devoid of presumption and relies solely upon what the Lord Himself has communicated to His people. As such, it is (to quote Martin Luther) "a living, daring confidence in God's grace" and His power to work out in her experience that which is impossible from man's point of view.

So we see that Ruth had met two important criteria that invariably precede the blessings we seek: (1) she had fulfilled the conditions of the covenant (note 1:16b), and (2) she was therefore in a position to claim its blessings.

When those twin truths are applied to us, they involve (1) living in obedience to God's revealed will, and (2) claiming by faith the blessings of His manifold provision for us (cf. 2 Pet. 1:4, KJV*).

Ruth lived obediently under the law. Her submission to it, however, was not the result of some legalistic imperative, but rather the response of an enlightened person to the grace of God. Second, by claiming the benefits of God's covenant she acted in faith, not knowing how matters would turn out.

Many of us fail on one of these points. On some occasions we may not have fulfilled the conditions before we claim the promise. Such acts, therefore, are presumptuous. At other times, when we have done all that

*King James Version.

God requires of us, we may wait patiently for the fulfillment of our prayers, not realizing that God expects us to claim His promised blessing. Fulfilling the conditions must precede the claiming of the promise, and the claiming of the promise must demonstrate the reality of our faith.

In her claim to the promise, Ruth's attitude was humble and discreet. She took appropriate precautions to ensure her safety, and when she stated her request it was brief, pointed, and picturesque. Her sincerity was evident, and Boaz responded with positive assurance.

NAOMI'S CHOICE

As we shift our focus from Ruth to Boaz, we find that he has been unaware of Naomi's plans. His introduction to those plans came suddenly as he awoke in the middle of the night to find a woman lying at his feet. D. B. MacDonald describes his mature reaction: "Boaz is shown quietly handling the situation like a gentleman, and not either as an old fool or a village lout. He may be countrified but he has dignity and restraint."[42]

After hearing Ruth's plea, Boaz readily acceded to her request. He also praised her for her loyalty to Naomi. Then he explained that, although he was indeed a near relative, there was one nearer of kin to Elimelech than he (3:12). Watson believes that statement explains why Boaz had not done more for Naomi and Ruth following their return from Moab. Boaz apparently did all he could to aid them, but within the bounds of social custom and in a way that would not cause Elimelech's "nearer kinsman" to take offense or lose face.[43]

With the assurance that he would do all he could to see Ruth taken care of, Boaz instructed her to lie down with him until morning (3:13).

FLESHLY INDULGENCE?

Many commentators believe that Boaz had intercourse with Ruth that night. They maintain that in that way he pledged himself to marry her. Others believe that that was part of Naomi's plan and that after seducing Ruth, Boaz felt obligated to redeem her.

The biblical writer chose his words carefully, and in his use of specific terms ruled out all possibility of moral impropriety. The Hebrew word *lûn*, "to pass the night," has latent within it the passage of time and does not concern itself with the manner in which the time was spent. If Boaz and Ruth had engaged in sexual relations on the threshing floor then *šākab*, "to lie [together], to sleep [together]" would have been used. *Lûn* is a word devoid of sexual connotations.

Naomi's confidence in Boaz's character, therefore, was fully justified. He and Ruth each possessed that intrinsic quality of character that enabled them to regulate their conduct without being ruled by their passions.[44]

We make a grave mistake, however, if we think of Boaz and Ruth following mechanically a well-rehearsed plot without being deeply involved in the dynamics of what was taking place. They were people with emotions like ours and they felt keenly the dramatic changes that the decision on the threshing floor would make in their lives.

THE EMOTION FACTOR

We may be sure that as Ruth lay on the floor at Boaz's feet she questioned in her mind whether Elimelech's "nearer relative" would exercise his option and take her as his concubine,[45] or whether he would give Boaz the right to marry her. And how would she handle the additional responsibilities of being a wife and still care for her mother-in-law? Naomi's proposal had given her no time to prepare for the new role that would soon be hers. And would she be able to bear a child? Ten years of marriage to Mahlon had failed to produce any offspring.

And what of Boaz? Certainly for him sleep was out of the question. What is revealed in chapter 4 of Ruth shows that, while on the threshing floor, he must have worked out a careful plan of action. It included protecting the rights of his kinsman by making him aware of the issues (cf. 4:3-4), while at the same time giving him the opportunity to decline gracefully if the kinsman felt that redeeming Ruth would be too great a burden. Boaz's thoughts were also of Elimelech, for he planned to care for Naomi as well. That would place him under a heavy financial burden. And if his plan was successful, if redeeming Ruth did become a reality— and with that he carefully rehearsed what he would say before the elders and the people of the city (cf. 4:9-10).

THE HAPPINESS QUOTIENT

Before leaving this passage, we should reflect on the ways in which love may be allowed to permeate our relationships.

THE PERSONAL DYNAMIC

We see first of all the free, open, and natural conversation of Naomi and Ruth. They had time for each other. They had fellowship together. Ruth shared with Naomi the events of the day, and Naomi shared with Ruth her counsel for the evening (cf. 2:21-22; 3:1-5).

Today we have become obsessed with *doing* rather than *being*. There are meetings to attend and responsibilities to assume. There is church and

PTA, civic functions and social gatherings, television programs and Little League, so much that we are on a treadmill. We seldom have leisure enough to sit down and talk with those we love—share our experiences, discuss our mutual interests, and be supportive of one another.

Accompanying this preoccupation with things has been an inability to listen to what others are saying. This is frequently linked with a corresponding inability to sense how others feel. Husbands have forgotten how to empathize truly with their wives, and wives have forgotten how to be supportive of their husbands. As the deterioration of the relationship continues, the channels of communication become blocked. Each becomes intent on fulfilling his or her own unmet needs. As time goes by, while they may continue to share the same address, the romance disappears from their marriage. They are more like strangers living under the same roof.

The same problem is frequently carried over into the relationship of parents with their children. Because building a quality relationship takes time and effort, many parents have drifted into patterns of behavior in which trite answers and superficial comments have replaced mature conversation. The result is that with their thoughts and feelings centering more and more on themselves, parents often do not heed their children's signals for help.[46]

The solution to these problems is illustrated for us by the pattern of fellowship and interaction established by Naomi and Ruth. Their lives were not free from anxiety, but their priorities were in order. They took time in a relaxed, unstructured way to communicate with each other. And as they did so, their love for one another was strengthened.

FORMULA FOR HAPPINESS

A second principle, closely related to the first, concerns happiness within a marriage and the kind of people who should marry. Marriage should only be entered into by those who are mature and share common beliefs and values: ones who are able to maintain a lasting relationship with the person they choose to marry, and who, if the marriage is to be a happy one, give evidence of their capacity to enjoy life. By far the commonest factor that causes problems in a marriage is the immaturity of one or both spouses.[47]

In Genesis 2:24 we are given the basis of the union of a man and a woman. A man must be prepared to "leave his father and mother" (implying his physical, intellectual, moral, and emotional maturity) and "cleave to his wife" (stressing the importance of unity arising out of their shared beliefs and values), so that the two of them may "become one flesh" (underscoring the need for sexual compatibility). Furthermore, in verse 25 we are told that Adam and Eve were "naked and [un]ashamed." That implies a perfect acceptance of each other's physiological and psychological differences. Anything less than personal maturity, the development of true unity, the cultivation of sexual compatibility, and the free acceptance of each other's individuality is an intimation of potential difficulty in a marriage.

Much time could be spent demonstrating from Ruth 1-3 that Boaz and Ruth were mature in themselves and brought that maturity to their marriage. Their relationship was also free from narcissistic tensions that would have tended to redirect their focus from each other to themselves. We also find Boaz and Ruth to be inwardly secure, regardless of their outward situation. They were both possessed of that quality of character that each found attractive in the other. Furthermore, their maturity may also be seen in their personal restraint. They were each able to control themselves in what might have become a highly compromising situation, and yet each felt free later on to express love in appropriate ways.

They were, therefore, in an ideal situation to marry, with all the potential for developing a lasting, mutually satisfying relationship.

HAPPINESS IS HOMEMADE

A final ingredient for a happy marriage is the ability to enjoy life. Whether a person has much or little in terms of material prosperity, the capacity to take a delight in what otherwise might be mundane and invest even the commonplace with significance makes a world of difference to a relationship. Those who possess such an outlook are always fun to be with and seem to grow better (rather than older) with the passing years.

In each scene we see Boaz's outgoing nature. In chapter 2 he cheerfully greeted the reapers, ate the noonday meal with them, and spoke kindly to a stranger. In chapter 3 he enjoyed the festivity of the harvest season, and as the text intimates, "his heart was 'good'" (3:7). And even when he would have the added responsibility of Naomi and Ruth, we may be sure that his ability to enjoy life would be as full as ever.

Ruth, too, shows that she was at heart a happy person. Throughout the book she was fully in touch with her emotions, yet never giving way to despondency. Her love and devotion to Naomi, assertion in providing for her mother-in-law's physical needs, and pleasant conversation are all indicative of her cheerful, loving nature. And as she would soon become Boaz's wife and later on bear him a son, we may again be sure that in the enjoyment of this "rest" she would bring to the home a wise, gracious, and loving spirit.

All of that brings us to an important conclusion. Regardless of what contemporary voices may be saying, marriage is the place where love finds its fullest expression and its greatest reward. Naomi realized that when she earnestly sought "rest" for Ruth. Various movements today are propagating different ideas about marriage—that conventional marriage is "restrictive," that traditional beliefs about marriage are as "outmoded as the horse and buggy," that being "just a housewife" programs a person for dependency, that couples who are "hooked on togetherness" will eventually find it to be destructive to the marital relationship, and that only by breaking out of the marriage "trap" can a person be free to mature as an individual.[48]

Those slanted terms do not describe marriage in the true sense of the word, but they have had an unsettling effect upon many people. Such views, however, are not shared by everyone, as one letter to the editor of the *Saturday Review* made clear:

> I am hopelessly behind the times. I'm a housewife. That means I spend three hours a day cooking and cleaning. The rest of the time I read, dream, study, listen to records, and paint. And, oh yes, I take care of my baby, which for some completely illogical reason is the warmest, most satisfying experience I've ever had—next to making my husband feel that he couldn't be happy without me.[49]

That is the kind of situation Naomi desired for Ruth, and it still holds greater promise of satisfaction for both husband and wife than any of the alternatives that have been suggested in recent years.

7

DEEDS OF THE RIGHTEOUS

(Ruth 3:14—4:6)

I came across a story recently that beautifully illustrates the kind of sensitivity we should have as we read God's Word. The writer, Dr. Richard Selzer, described an incident that took place during his medical internship.

One day as he passed the bulletin board of the hospital, he saw a notice. It advised those on the staff that Dr. Yashi Dhonden, an eminent Tibetan physician, would make his rounds on a particular morning.

Such an opportunity was not to be missed, and on that morning Dr. Selzer joined the clutch of whitecoats a little before 6:00 A.M. and waited. At precisely 6:00 Dr. Dhonden appeared. He was short, golden-skinned, rotund, and dressed in a sleeveless robe of saffron and maroon.

Dr. Dhonden bowed to his colleagues as he entered. He then asked to see the patient who had been selected for examination. The patient, of course, had been awakened a short time before and advised of what was going to take place.

As he entered the patient's room, Dr. Dhonden noticed her spirit of compliance—the attitude of resignation that frequently is shown by a chronically ill person. He said nothing, but walked to the bed and for a long time gazed at her, yet not so as to cause her embarrassment. No physical sign or obvious symptom gave him a clue to the nature of her ailment. Then he took her hand in both of his and, with his eyes closed, felt her pulse. His concentration was obvious. His rapt attention made him oblivious to the passing of time.

At last he straightened, gently placed the woman's hand back on the bed and stepped backward. Speaking through an interpreter he asked for the specimen that had been taken earlier. That he likewise examined, then turned to leave.

Before Dr. Dhonden could pass through the door, the woman raised her head off the pillow and said, "Thank you, doctor." She evidently felt that this Asian physician understood her suffering.

When he was alone with the other doctors, Dr. Dhonden gave his diagnosis. Little was lost through the interpreter. He spoke in pictures and symbols. He described winds coursing through the body of an unborn child and of currents breaking against barriers. Long before the patient was born, a "wind" had "blown open a gate" between the chambers of her heart, that must never be opened. Through that opening now charged the full "waters" of her bloodstream.

Without elaborate tests, X-rays, or exploratory surgery, Dr. Dhonden had diagnosed congenital heart disease: an interventricular septal defect with resultant heart failure.[1]

Sensitive and Honest

In the same way that the Tibetan doctor was able to become vitally in tune with his patient's body and intimately aware of her condition, so we too should develop an unhurried understanding of what God is saying to us through His Word. That will not happen all at once. Each one of us, however, can develop the skills we need if we will but persevere.

In our present story, for example, we notice:

- the obvious empathy between Ruth and Boaz. Ruth sensed intuitively Boaz's concern lest she be seen on the threshing floor and took the initiative by rising early "before one could recognize another" (3:14). Boaz sensed her concern. He approved of her action and said, "Let it not be known that a woman came to the threshing floor."

- God's evident involvement in the events that took place at the gate. Boaz had just made himself comfortable when, "*Behold,* there is the very kinsman of whom he had spoken" (4:1). One such reference (i.e., "Behold") might not arouse much interest on our part, but this device of drawing our attention to events as they are transpiring has been used repeatedly by the writer (2:4; 3:8; 4:1).

- that the kinsman of Naomi is not named (4:1). This does not mean that neither Boaz nor the recorder of these events knew his name. Rather it implies that the writer used this tactful device so that descendants of the individual might not be offended. From our point of view, the unnamed kinsman passes off the page of Scripture and soon fades from our minds.

- the way Boaz graciously yet firmly took control of the meeting at the gate ("Turn aside, sit down here" v. 2); his control of his own emotions, which was so evident in his timing (e.g., in not mentioning the reason for the meeting until he was ready); and the way he offered his relative a way to save face before the elders and all the people ("Buy [the field] before those sitting here . . . but if you will not redeem [the field], tell me . . . [and] I will redeem it" v. 4). All this points to the maturity and wisdom of the one whom Naomi had selected as the best husband for Ruth.

- clues to the motive of the unnamed kinsman. His intentions become apparent when we consider how readily he wished to add to his own estate ("I will redeem it," v. 4). However, when he learned that Ruth was also involved in the "purchase," he quickly changed his mind. That becomes very evident when we observe the repetition of "for" in verse 6 (*lî*, "for myself," contrasted with *leka*, "for yourself").[2] Notice also the subtle stress of his words: "*I* cannot . . . lest *I* . . . *my* right . . . *I* cannot." He apparently thought only of himself.

New Day Dawning

With renewed sensitivity, therefore, we read Ruth 3:14-18:

And Ruth lay at his feet[3] until the morning, and she[4] arose before a man could discern his neighbor.[5] And Boaz said, "Do not let it be known that a [lit., the[6]] woman came to the threshing floor." And he said, "Give me the cloak which is on you, and hold on to it."[7] And Ruth kept hold on it, and he measured six [*seāh*][8] of barley [into it] and laid it on her.[9] Then he[10] went into the city.

And Ruth came to her mother-in-law, and Naomi said, "How did things go, my daughter?" [lit., Who are you?].[11] And Ruth told her all that Boaz [lit., the man] had done to her. And she said, "He gave me these six [*seāh*] of barley, for he said, 'You shall not go empty to your mother-in-law.'"[12] And Naomi said, "Sit, my daughter, until you shall know how [the] matter[13] falls [i.e., how everything turns out], for the man will not rest until he has completed the matter today."

SACRED VALUES

Being a woman of maturity and believing in the sanctity of marriage, Ruth lay at Boaz's feet (not by his side!) until the first blush of dawn upon the hills heralded the approach of a new day. Then, wishing to protect Boaz from any unnecessary scandal, she arose so as to leave the threshing floor before any of the men who had slept there became aware of her presence.

Boaz too arose. He was a righteous man, but he was also sufficiently in touch with the seamy side of human nature to know how readily those of the city would seize upon a seeming indiscretion to tarnish Ruth's character.

Such wisdom is not often found among generous, large-hearted people. They frequently expect people to act toward them with the same magnanimity they show others, and their very honesty makes them vulnerable.

Boaz, therefore, serves as a good model of the practical wisdom we should apply to our own situations. His conduct shows that it is easier to prevent a problem than to solve it after it has arisen.

TANGIBLE COMMITMENT

Boaz sent Ruth back to the city, but took care that she not return to Naomi empty-handed. He asked her to take off her mantle and hold one end of it. He then placed in it six *seāh* of barley. Because the quantity of barley was such that Ruth could not lift it *and* satisfactorily adjust it for carrying, Boaz set it upon her. He then allowed her to return to Naomi.

Two questions concern us: (1) why did Boaz feel that it was necessary to send Naomi a gift, and (2) is there anything significant in the fact that in Ruth 1:21 Naomi had complained of returning to Bethlehem "empty" and here Boaz says, "Do not return *empty* to your mother-in-law"?

First, it seems as if the gift of barley was a pledge to Naomi, some tangible assurance that Boaz would indeed redeem her and Ruth. As such, it served to illustrate the generosity of a righteous man who was prepared to do more than the law required of him.

Second, the reminder of Naomi's situation underscored the grace of God. He had brought Naomi back to Judah stripped of her wealth and deprived of her family. But in response to her renewed trust in Him, He was in the process of making provision for her future needs. She would not know want or suffer privation again. And in time He would also give her a son (cf. 4:13*b* with vv. 15-17*a*).

A BIT OF HISTORY

Bible translation history was made with verse 15. The Hebrew text reads, "And *he* (Boaz) went into the city." Most of our translations follow an amended text and have *Ruth* going to the city.

The first edition of the Authorized (King James) Version, published in 1611, followed the Masoretic (Hebrew) Text. It became known as the

"He" Bible. In the same year a second printing was called for, and in that edition the text was changed to read, "And *she* went in to the city." That printing became known as the "She" Bible.[14]

Scholars are still undecided about which translation is to be preferred. The point is not of vital importance. We have chosen, however, to adhere to the reading of the Hebrew text. Boaz filled Ruth's mantle with barley and then went into the city. There he prepared for the events of the day. That left the writer free to conclude the chapter as it began, with Naomi and Ruth.

LEARNING TO TRUST GOD

Ruth returned to Naomi with the six measures of barley[15] and shared with her all that had transpired during the night. Both women were concerned whether the nearer kinsman would exercise the rights of a redeemer, buy the field, and marry Ruth.

Realizing that nothing was to be gained by fretfully pacing the floor, Naomi counseled Ruth to sit still and await the outcome of the events that would soon unfold at the city gate.

Such times of waiting frequently are productive of anxiety and destructive of faith. It is hard to wait. Tension mounts and we feel that we should be doing something.

Naomi's recommendation to Ruth was based on her knowledge of Boaz's character. She knew him to be a person who was as good as his word. He was proactive and decisive; he would not rest until the issue had been resolved. And because the whole affair ultimately rested in God's hands, there was no need to fret or become overly anxious. Trust is the antidote to anxiety, and sitting still and waiting was the best course of action for Ruth to follow.

A PROMISE TO KEEP

As the scene moves to the gate of the city, the writer stresses Boaz's character:

> Then Boaz went up to the gate[16] and sat there; and, behold the near kinsman [i.e., the close relative] of whom he had spoken was passing by.[17] And Boaz said to him, "Turn aside,[18] sit down here." And he turned aside and sat down. And Boaz took ten men of the elders of the city,[19] and said, "Sit down here." And they sat down.
> And Boaz said to the near kinsman, "Naomi, who has returned from the fields of Moab, will sell[20] the portion of the field which [belonged] to our brother Elimelech. And I said, 'I will uncover your ear[21] [i.e., inform you], saying, "Acquire it before those sitting [here] and before the elders of my

people." If you will redeem [it], redeem [it]; but if he[22] will not redeem [it], tell me so that I may know; for there is no one apart from you to redeem [it], and I[23] [am] after you.'"

And he said "I will redeem [it]."

And Boaz said, "In the day of your acquiring[24] the field from the hand of Naomi, you must also acquire Ruth the Moabitess, the wife of the dead, to raise up the name of the dead upon his inheritance."[25]

And the near kinsman said, "I am not able to redeem [it] for myself, lest I ruin my own inheritance.[26] You redeem [it] for yourself; you [take] my right to redeem it, for I am not able to redeem [it]." [4:1-6]

FORGOTTEN FACES

While Ruth and Naomi waited patiently at home, not knowing how their future would be affected by the day's events, Boaz went up to the gate through which the citizens passed on their way to the fields.

Just as Boaz took a seat within the wall, the other relative of Elimelech passed by. Boaz called out to him, *Peloni ʾalomoni,* signifying that he had something of a legal nature to discuss with him. Boaz courteously asked his kinsman to take a seat and then impaneled ten trustworthy elders of the city. When everything was ready, Boaz opened the proceedings by informing his relative of Naomi's decision to sell the property that belonged to Elimelech. He reminded his kinsman that the latter's relationship to Elimelech was closer than his (Boaz's) own. Boaz also assured the man of his willingness to purchase the land should the nearer kinsman not be in a position to do so.

The unnamed kinsman quickly agreed to buy the land. His "*I* will redeem it" is emphatic.

NO TRADE-OFFS

The subtle emphases of the Hebrew text have led different students of the Word to probe for the motivating force behind Boaz's kinsman's marked willingness to buy Naomi's property.[27]

He could have excused himself from any form of levirate[28] (i.e., brother-in-law) responsibility on the grounds that it did not conform to the letter of the law (cf. Lev. 25:23-28), but the kinsman tacitly admitted the legitimacy of Boaz's recommendation. The right of redemption was for the benefit of the poor. Did this *gōʾēl* stand to gain from the transaction?

The answer he gave to Boaz seems to point to his inherent selfishness. In Israel those who sold property had it restored to them at the year of Jubilee. However, if they had a kinsman who would buy it back for them, it was to be purchased from the buyer and restored to the owner. In that way the property would always remain in the family and practical help was extended to those in need.

Naomi, however, was a widow; her sons were dead. She was also beyond child-bearing years. For the relative to purchase the field from her meant that the land would become his without any fear of its being bought back (i.e., redeemed) by any of Naomi's descendants.

The opportunity presented to the kinsman appeared to offer him the chance of *adding* to his present possessions with Naomi having no legal way of ever recovering the land.

ATMOSPHERE OF SUSPENSE

As we return to the story, we need to remember that the writer of the book of Ruth is painting graphic word pictures for his readers. It does no injustice to Scripture if we believe that those who first listened to the story, or had it read to them, were hoping that Boaz and Ruth would eventually marry. Now, however, all seemed lost. Those who were anticipating a happy ending to the story have heard the unnamed kinsman say, "I will redeem the land." They knew that Ruth was bound up in the transaction. They feared that the "villain" might go off with the "heroine" after all.

Boaz had acted in his integrity and given his relative the right of first refusal. Has his honesty resulted in his personal loss?

Boaz, however, still had something to relate to his kinsman. He said in effect, "On the day that you buy the field from the hand of Naomi, you must also take the hand of Ruth [in marriage] and raise up the name of the dead on his plot of ground" (4:5).

FALL OF THE DOMINO

With a remarkably rapid change of heart, Elimelech's relative replied, "I cannot redeem it for myself, lest I jeopardize my own inheritance. Redeem it for yourself. You take my right of redemption, for I cannot redeem it" (4:6).

But why the sudden change in attitude? Keil and Delitzsch explain the would-be redeemer's changed motivation:

If he [had] acquired the field by redemption as his own permanent property, he would have increased by so much his own possessions in land. But if he should marry Ruth, the field so redeemed would belong to the son whom he would beget through her, and he would therefore have parted with the money that he had paid for the redemption merely for the son of Ruth, so that he would have withdrawn a certain amount of capital from his own possession, and to that extent have detracted from its worth.[29]

FLAWED HERITAGE

It seems ironic that this Bethlehemite, who was so concerned about preserving his heritage, has been forgotten. Cox states:

> It is a curious comment on his narrow, selfish ambition, that, of this man who was bent on preserving his name and fame, who would run no risk of having his name cut from his place, neither Israel nor the world even so much as remembers [his] mere name. He is unnamed in the very Book which recounts his story; we know him simply as the "anonymous kinsman"; while Boaz, who had no such selfish ambition, who held that in every nation they who trust God and work righteousness are acceptable with Him, lives on forever on the sacred page, and is enrolled, together with Ruth, in the pedigree of Him whose Name is above every name.[30]

The facelessness of Elimelech's kinsman reminds me of something I once read about a famous painting by John Singer Sargent (1856-1925). He was approached by Elizabeth Garrett, the founder of Johns Hopkins University Medical School, to paint a group portrait of the four doctors who had brought such renown to the institution: Welch, Halstead, Osler, and Kelly.

From the very beginning, Dr. Welch did not get along with Sargent. He complained that Sargent called them all "Kelly," and objected to the way they were told to pose. Dr. Welch so angered Sargent that he was told he would be painted so that his facial features would gradually fade and he would not be remembered by posterity.

The painting of "The Four Doctors" still hangs (I am told) in Johns Hopkins Medical School, but the face of Dr. William Henry Welsh is steadily fading. Those who walk the halls of that prestigious university can no longer discern what Dr. Welsh looked like.

Those who give of themselves in the service of others are remembered (as Boaz is to this day) for those qualities of character that truly made them great.

SINGLED OUT

Our primary concern ought to be to learn as much as we can from these verses. They illustrate for us, as Watson has pointed out, that "A good man will have everything done with perfect openness and honor and will stand by the result whether it meets his hopes or disappoints them."[31]

TOO RIGHTEOUS?

As we reflect on the passage we cannot help but notice the integrity and discretion of the one whom Naomi had singled out as a husband for Ruth. Boaz was frank in his approach and straightforward in his business dealings. He was also aware of the social customs of his people. At no time did he give offense, either by word or deed. His relative had the prior claim to redeem Naomi's land, and Boaz not only advised him of his right but also recommended that he exercise it. All his actions were characterized by a sense of justice too little found among God's people today.

THE MATTER OF DISCERNMENT

We notice that Boaz was also discreet. In our day he illustrates the kind of person who would put important things in writing. In his day he obtained ten reliable witnesses to attest what took place. He did not select people of inferior standing in the community, whose word might be altered with a suitable bribe. Instead, he chose people whose trustworthiness and knowledge were well established. These he summoned to witness all that transpired.

THE MIX-UP OVER EMOTIONS

There can be little doubt that Boaz wished to marry Ruth. She appealed to him. The qualities of her character matched his own. So he faced a tension between his personal desires and his familial duty. How was this tension to be resolved? Certainly not by ignoring the rights of others or having a clandestine relationship. The tension was resolved by doing the right thing in the right way.

Boaz's integrity kept his task in perspective and his desires in their place. As a result, his emotions did not obstruct his reason. He could make the basic issues known to his kinsman and then, because he was able to control the pace as well as the content of the meeting, he could advise his relative of the responsibility that accompanied the purchase of the land—marriage to Ruth.

WHAT EXPERIENCE TELLS US

The kind of practical righteousness demonstrated by Boaz is not often found in Christian circles. We often lack patience, are selfish, and play "political" games in order to get what we want. Our thoughts and desires are centered on ourselves. We find it easy to excuse our actions. We blame our hang-ups on our parents, our materialism on the economy, our inordinate desire for things on social trends, and secretly excuse our conduct by comparing ourselves with other people. We conclude, "I'm not so bad after all."

It is only as we open our hearts to the searching light of Holy Scripture and compare our conduct with what is revealed there that we realize how mercenary, self-centered, and ungodly we may have become.

What then are we to do if we would be characterized by the kind of practical righteousness illustrated by a man like Boaz?

I believe that the answer is found in Boaz's God-ward orientation. He lived out his life—faced the effects of a lengthy famine, achieved a reputation for his ability to lead Bethlehem's band of militia, had a positive influence on his workers, took the initiative when necessary, and conducted himself honorably in a variety of circumstances—conscious all the while that God's eye was upon him. It is no wonder that in crucial situations the uprightness of his character shone as clearly as the sun's rays on the shimmering waters of a lake.

We too may exhibit the same moral probity and practical maturity. We need to remember, however, that the bricks of character are laid one by one. In the same way that character takes time to develop, so does the kind of maturity and instinctively right conduct found in a person such as Boaz.

The place to begin is with a renewed commitment of our entire life to the Lord. With that foundation, we can build a consistent pattern of doing the right thing in the right way. Self-restraint and (on occasion) self-sacrifice will be needed. To those will be added the importance of fulfilling our moral duties (as Boaz did), along with the ability to speak the truth in love to our neighbor.

Many more lessons can be drawn from this passage. The more we ponder it and internalize its message, the greater will be our growth toward spiritual maturity.

8

How We Should Live

(Ruth 4:7-13)

One of the evidences of spiritual maturity is graciousness.

It is inevitable that a person becomes like the thing or things he worships. That was true of people living in Old Testament times, and it is true of us today. Human nature has not changed. The things we covet (i.e., wealth, success, popularity, influence, possessions of one sort or another) are spoken of in the New Testament as "idols" (cf. Col. 3:5) that we worship. An eclipse takes place—one that may last for many years or even a lifetime.

The effect of the worship of "other gods" has been dramatized, for example, in Robert Wilder's seedy portrayal of the lust for power and wealth, *Flamingo Road.*[1]

By way of contrast, the more we are taken up with God and His goodness,[2] the more we take on His likeness (cf. 2 Cor. 3:18). And one of the characteristics of such growth is graciousness. God is a God of grace (cf. Ex. 19:4; 20:6; Deut. 7:7ff.). He delights in demonstrating His lovingkindness to those who are the recipients of His grace. This doctrine is filled out in the New Testament in the Lord Jesus Christ, who is the personification of the grace of God (John 1:17), the express image of God's Person (Heb. 1:3).

We come to understand, therefore, that whether in the Old Testament

117

or the New, God deals graciously with His people. And as He is, so we should be in the world.

In our study of the book of Ruth we have already come across the word *ḥesed*. It is a term used to describe God's steadfast love. The Hebrew scholar of a generation past, William Gesenius, believed that *ḥesed* characterized an "eager and ardent desire by which anyone is led."[3]

In the Old Testament, *ḥesed* is frequently translated "lovingkindness." It involves a relationship on the basis of which acts of kindness are performed. Such relationships can exist between peers (e.g., David and Jonathan), a king and his subjects (e.g., David and the people of Israel), God and a nation, or between God and an individual.

The basis of God's relationships is always His firm, persistent, and steadfast love. That does not mean He cannot or will not chasten those whom He loves (Heb. 12:8-11). It does mean that when chastening becomes necessary, it is done with our good as the goal. Our response to God's grace should be twofold: (1) we should respond in loving obedience to His will, and (2) demonstrate the same kind of *ḥesed* in our relationships with others. As we have seen, that was the basis of Naomi's home in Moab (1:8), and it does not surprise us that Orpah and Ruth loved her.

In the New Testament, the word used to describe this attitude of God toward us is *charis* ("grace"). It is one of the great words of our Christian vocabulary. *Charis* is connected with the word that means "joy" *(chara)*. Grace really means "that which causes joy." Only in the presence of the Lord is there fullness of joy (Ps. 16:11), and so salvation—which is by grace and quite apart from works (Eph. 2:8-9)—is the act of God whereby, on account of His love for us, He takes us out to the helpless state in which sin holds us captive, releases us, and restores us to a right standing before Him. All this is done by God and is based solely on the sacrificial death of Christ on our behalf. This new experience of grace is designed to make possible our experience of "fullness of joy."[4]

MANIFESTATIONS OF GRACE

In the fourth chapter of Ruth, following Elimelech's kinsman's refusal to redeem both Ruth *and* the land (4:6), the writer provides us with an explanation of what took place at the gate of the city. The book of Deuteronomy states:

> But if the man does not desire to take his brother's wife, then his brother's wife shall go up to the gate to the elders and say, "My husband's brother refuses to establish a name for his brother in Israel; he is not willing to perform the duty of a husband's brother to me" . . . . Then his brother's wife shall come to him in

the sight of the elders, and pull his sandal off his foot and spit in his face. . . .
And in Israel his name shall be called, "The house of him whose sandal is
removed." [Deut. 25:7-10, NASB]

The writer of Ruth explains: "And this [was] formerly [done][5] in Israel
concerning redemption, and concerning the exchange [of property], to
confirm[6] every matter: a man would draw off[7] his sandal and give [it] to
his neighbor; and this was the attestation[8] in Israel. And the kinsman said
to Boaz, 'You acquire for yourself.' And he[9] drew off his sandal" (4:7-8).

In these verses we notice two important aspects of grace. Others will be
observed in succeeding verses. For the present we see (1) the gracious
maturity of the writer, and (2) the kindness of the elders.

The writer has been steadily developing our interest in Boaz and Ruth.
They were noble in character, mature in their personhood, and in every
way commended themselves to those who admire the best in other
people. It would have been easy, therefore, for him to speak con-
temptuously of anyone opposing Boaz and Ruth or doing them harm.

When Elimelech's relative refused to redeem the poverty-stricken
widows, we might have expected some evidence of the writer's disdain.
Scripture had already established a precedent that such a person be
exposed to public shame and referred to by the unflattering name of
"Baresole." The narrator, however, treats the relative of Elimelech with
gentleness. He continues to refer to him as gō 'ēl, "redeemer" (4:8).

Second, we observe the gracious kindness of the elders. They
permitted the unnamed kinsman to take off his shoe and give it to Boaz
without summoning Ruth to their meeting and having her humiliate him
before the residents of the city.

Was their act one of weakness? Did they tolerate the flouting of God's
law because they lacked the conviction to uphold it? Were they guilty of
compromise? It would appear that they were not. In the presence of
righteousness, the conduct of the unrighteous is exposed. Before men of
integrity, a person whose actions are prompted by ulterior motives stands
rebuked. His shame, therefore, arises from within himself. His own heart
condemns him. Only where righteousness is not practiced consistently by
those in positions of responsibility is it necessary to insist upon the letter
of the law.

SIGNIFICANT GESTURE

Elimelech's kinsman does not lack for critics. It is hard to find a single
writer who speaks well of him. Perhaps the reason he appears in such a
bad light is that he is cast next to Boaz. As a result, the imperfections of
his character stand out clearly. For an illustration of that, note the

gracelessness of his reply to Boaz in verse 8. The Hebrew conveys the terseness of his response: "Buy for yourself."

"Buy what?" we may ask. Is Ruth so contemptible a creature that she is unworthy of a name? Is such disdain for a human being justifiable? Why should a person who has a few moments ago responded with alacrity by saying, "I will buy Naomi's plot of ground" now respond in such an abrasive manner?

The answer to this kinsman's gracelessness seems to lie in his being caught on the horns of a dilemma. And there were plenty of people present to witness his discomfort! He had been trapped by his own greed. When he learned from Boaz that Naomi was compelled to sell her land (and knowing that she had no heirs to reclaim it from him), he readily agreed to perform the duty of a *gō ʾēl*.

But by assuming the responsibilities of a redeemer in one area (i.e., the "redemption" of the land Naomi was selling), he tacitly placed himself under all legislation applying to a kinsman—one of the functions of which concerned "brother-in-law (levirate) marriage." When Boaz mentioned his need to marry Ruth (4:5), he quickly backed off.[10] There was no commercial advantage to be gained by marrying Ruth. However, he must have sensed inwardly how his own emotions had betrayed him, and so he said tersely to Boaz, "Buy for yourself."

Taylor sums up his attitude: "One thing . . . is very clear, namely, that his whole thought was about his own inheritance, and thus selfishness was at the root of his decision."[11]

Ruth was not present at the gate and the elders of the city did not summon her. The kinsman, however, voluntarily removed his sandal and gave it to Boaz to avoid further public humiliation. By doing so he transferred to Boaz his right to act as the redeemer of Ruth and Naomi.

The significance of that act has been described by Morison. "He who sold land, or surrendered his right to act as a kinsman in buying land, intimated by the symbolic act of taking off his shoe, and handing it to his friend, that he freely gave up his right to walk on the soil, in favor of the person who had acquired possession."[12]

LETTER OF THE LAW

With the right to act as Naomi's and Ruth's redeemer legally assigned to him, Boaz turned to the elders and all the people and said:

> [You are] witnesses[13] today that I have acquired all that [belonged] to Elimelech, and all that [belonged] to Chilion and Mahlon,[14] from the hand of Naomi; and also Ruth the Moabitess,[15] the wife of Mahlon, I have acquired for myself to be my wife, to raise up the name of the dead upon his inheritance, so

that the name of the dead shall not be cut off from among his brothers, or from the gate of his people [lit., place];[16] you are witnesses today. [4:9-10]

The events of the morning had been very taxing for Boaz. He had consistently done what was right, regardless of his personal preferences. Now in a carefully worded legal statement he outlined all that he proposed to do for Elimelech's widow and daughter-in-law.

Boaz's emotion was evident in his words, yet his feelings were under control. His graciousness may be seen in his refraining from drawing any unpleasant contrast between his conduct and that of Elimelech's other kinsman. Instead, Boaz carefully outlined all that he was acquiring and clearly stated his intention to take Ruth as his wife. He did not forget his obligations and affirmed before all present that their first son would inherit Mahlon's estate and perpetuate his name.

MORE THAN GOOD INTENTIONS

As we consider Boaz's activity at the gate of the village, let us observe the degree to which he illustrates the principle of grace. George Knight reminds us that

> if a mere man, a creature of God, could behave in the manner described, and had indeed by his action exhibited the power to redeem an outcast and bring her into fellowship with the living God, then two things could be said of the Creator of Boaz—(1) God must feel at least as compassionate towards all the Ruths of Moab and of Babylon and of every other land as his creature Boaz felt towards Ruth; (2) God must actually be a God of redemption, with the desire and the power to redeem all outcasts into fellowship with himself.[17]

BRIDGING THE GAP

Boaz's role as a *kinsman-redeemer* has caused many Bible scholars to see a parallel with the Lord Jesus Christ.

First, according to Leviticus 25:23ff. and Deuteronomy 25:7-10 the redeemer must be a near relative. When that truth is compared to the teaching of the New Testament, we come to understand the necessity for Christ's incarnation. He needed to share our humanity (cf. Heb. 2:14), and so He became our Kinsman "according to the flesh" in order that He might redeem us from sin.

Second, a kinsman in Israel could not exercise the right of redemption if he himself were in debt, had sold part of his own estate, or were too poor to do so. That brings into focus the reason for the temptation of Jesus. Through His temptation He demonstrated that His "estate" (i.e., His Person) had not been mortgaged to sin. He was free from both a sin nature and sinful practices (Heb. 4:15). He could say to His disciples,

"The prince of this world comes and has no power over Me" (John 14:30). Christ was therefore able to perform the part of our Kinsman and redeem us from our bankrupt state.

Finally, Boaz illustrates that the kinsman must be willing to pay the price necessary to buy back the mortgaged inheritance of another. That could only be done at personal cost. The Lord Jesus willingly went to the cross to accomplish our redemption (John 10:15b, 18a; 1 Pet. 3:18).

All of this further highlights the New Testament doctrine of redemption. It pictures a slave-market where people are enslaved by sin (Rom. 7:14). From this position we are bought by Christ and then released. Sin, however, has been committed, and sin is always viewed as being committed against God. The ransom must therefore be paid to Him. Christ paid the price for our redemption; God has declared Himself satisfied (1 John 2:2), and on the basis of Christ's work for us God can now deal with us in grace. And we in gratitude can render Him loving service.

TIMELY BENEDICTION

Boaz's willingness to redeem Naomi and marry Ruth evoked the praise of all who witnessed the proceedings. They gave a spontaneous expression of their admiration in the form of a benediction.[18]

> May *Yahweh* grant that the woman who has come[19] into your house [be] as Rachel and as Leah,[20] both of whom[21] built the house of Israel; and may you achieve wealth [lit., act worthily][22] in Ephrath and become famous [lit., (be) called a name][23] in Bethlehem. And may your house be like the house of Perez whom Tamar bore to Judah, through the seed which *Yahweh* shall give you of this young woman.[24] [4:11-12]

The people and the elders responded to Boaz by affirming their status as witnesses and by pronouncing a blessing upon him and Ruth.

MISPLACED PRIORITIES

It is hard to imagine a more uncomfortable position than the one occupied by Elimelech's unnamed kinsman. To be desirous of those things that would enhance his own prestige and reputation, and then to hear the elders bestowing their accolades on Boaz and wishing him prosperity and fame must have caused the kinsman considerable personal discomfort (if not outright envy).

He reminds us, however, of those whose thoughts and actions are controlled by worldly considerations. They may prosper for a time, but they are seldom satisfied. Their possessions are never quite sufficient; their crops are never quite as good as they had hoped; their work never quite earns for them the recognition they believe they deserve; and as they grow older, their thoughts are frequently dominated by what might have been.

How much better to live as Boaz did, do what is right, and enjoy the blessing of God upon one's life.

THE INVOCATION OF BLESSING

One unique characteristic of Judaism and Christianity is that they possess the power to bless. As mentioned earlier, in pagan religions power is derived from the ability to punish or curse.[25] A study of the word *bārak*, "to bless," in the Old Testament shows that the blessing might take the form of a benediction (cf. Num. 6:23-27), be an act of worship (Ps. 103), or transmit something from someone who is greater to someone of lesser status or ability (Heb. 7:7, referring to Gen. 14:19).

The term "to bless" *(bārak)* is closely related to the word for "knee," *(berek)*. The connection may involve "bowing the knee" in acknowledgment of God's past favors (Gen. 24:28; Deut. 8:10). The Old Testament sees the verb and its derivatives "blessing" and "blessedness" as having God as the source. The blessings of His covenant extend to every area of life (Deut. 28:3-6) and are attributable to His gracious character (cf. Deut. 23:5).[26]

Because God's rule over His creation is through people whom He has chosen, He has delegated to His representatives the power to pronounce blessing in His name.[27] That is why Isaac's blessing of Jacob and Esau (Gen. 27) or Jacob's blessing of his sons (Gen. 48) became, in a sense, a prophecy of them and their descendants. That is also why Eli could promise Hannah that her prayer would be answered (1 Sam. 1:9-18, 20).

As the responsibility for acting on God's behalf was diversified, the ability to bless people in the name of the Lord (i.e., as if God were present) was shared among different kinds of leaders (cf. Num. 11:16-25). Because this gift came more and more to be identified with the Holy Spirit, we see how our indwelling and filling by the Spirit of God places us in a position to be a blessing to, and confer blessing upon, other people.

We should not forget, however, that blessing is a gracious activity of God on our behalf whereby He enriches our lives by supplying us with that which we lack.

DAYS OF AUSTERITY?

It is also interesting to notice that the blessing of the elders of the city and the general benediction of the people contain a prayer that the Lord will grant Boaz prosperity.

We have insufficient evidence for dogmatism, but must admit to the strong probability that Boaz was not a wealthy man. When we remember that his financial resources had been severely depleted during the years of famine (as had everyone else's), and that in all probability he already had a wife and family, we begin to see why the people of Bethlehem desired that he "act worthily (i.e., become prosperous) in Ephratah, and become famous in Bethlehem."[28]

TOGETHER AT LAST

Boaz made his way to the humble cottage of Naomi with the blessing of the people of Bethlehem still sounding in his ears. From what transpires later on (4:16) we conclude that Boaz took both women to his home.

We are not told what kind of reception Naomi and Ruth received from the other members of Boaz's household. They had only learned of Ruth's claim on Boaz when he returned from the threshing floor shortly before dawn. Adjustments are never easy to make, particularly when they mean a change in one's life-style. We can only hope that Boaz's household acted as graciously toward Ruth and Naomi as Boaz, the elders, and the people had done. The biblical text merely states, "And Boaz took Ruth, and she became his wife, and he went in to her; and *Yahweh* gave her conception [i.e., enabled her to conceive], and she gave birth to a son" (4:13).

Ruth had not had much time to prepare herself mentally or emotionally for marriage to Boaz, but her experience does not provide an excuse for young people to rush into marriage. The old axiom "Marry in haste, repent at leisure" needs no further ratification.

Ruth's marriage to Boaz does illustrate the importance of *being* the right mate rather than trying to find the right one. Of course, she would have had to make adjustments as part of the household of Boaz. However, we may be sure that she brought to the situation the same maturity and graciousness that has characterized her throughout the story.

It is also important to reflect on God's involvement in Ruth's marriage. A short time before, Naomi had despaired of Ruth's ability to find "rest" among Naomi's people. She had recommended that each daughter-in-law return to her mother's home and seek a husband among her own people (1:8-9, 11-16). But that which seemed utterly impossible to achieve from a human standpoint, God in His infinite wisdom and steadfast love had accomplished for Ruth in an alien land.

A further observation on God's gracious involvement in the marriage of Ruth and Boaz has been made by Morris. He points out that "the son that was born is regarded as God's gift."[29] He then reminds us that "throughout this book there is the consistent thought that God is over all and works out His will. We have seen that the elders and others regarded children as God's gift (4:12) and we see the same thought now from the author."[30] Though Ruth had remained childless throughout her first marriage, she was now able to bear a son. Such an occurrence must surely have been evidence of God's blessing.[31]

THE SOURCE

Considering the numerous illustrations of God's providential care and provision found throughout the book of Ruth, we are led sooner or later to search for their underlying cause. Did He single out Ruth and graciously elect her to be the recipient of His favor while denying the same blessings to others?

That question is more than an academic one. Its answer spells the difference between hope and disillusionment for each of us. The writer has shown repeatedly that there is a definite relationship between fidelity and its reward. Emphasis has been placed on Ruth's piety; her loyalty to Naomi (1:8; 2:11; 3:10), which involved obedience to the revealed will of God; her diligence in caring for Naomi (2:2, 7); her obedience and her moral integrity.

The blessings of God are the result of a relationship. In this connection it is important for us to notice the name for God used most frequently throughout the book: *Yahweh*. It is only one of the many names for God, and is specifically used of Him in relation to His covenant with the people of Israel.

When the emphasis on relationship (stressed repeatedly by the use of the name *Yahweh*) is coupled with the practice of obedience, we have the key elements to the secret of spiritual growth and the enjoyment of God's blessings. He desires a relationship with us. He has demonstrated His lovingkindness and steadfast desire for what is best for us. If our response to Him is positive and characterized by obedience, then we too may enjoy the evidences of God's grace.

Reflecting upon these incidents Taylor said,

Not every story that begins so sadly as this did has so sweet and pleasant an ending. Not always are virtue, piety, constancy, and self-sacrifice so visibly rewarded upon the earth. But we are not on that account to think less of the providence of God; for virtue is not to be pursued because of its reward, and right is to be done for its own sake—nay, rather, for the sake of God. Then, when the end shall come . . . we shall see the vindication of Jehovah.[32]

9

NAOMI'S RECOMPENSE

(Ruth 4:14-22)

The name of John Calvin is revered by students of Scripture all over the world. Whether or not we agree with all that he wrote, the fact is that theologians quote extensively from his *Institutes of the Christian Religion* and sociologists study his system of ethics. Politicians analyze the impact of his principles of democracy, and historians evaluate the effect of his influence on succeeding generations. It has become popular in our day to publish biographies of him, issue new translations of his works, and compile bibliographies listing those works.

Few of us who laud the great accomplishments of "the genius of Geneva,"[1] pause to recollect that he was not always held in such high esteem. To show their contempt for him some of the people of Geneva called their dogs "Calvin." When they saw him passing by, they would call, "Calvin, Calvin," and as he turned in their direction they would stoop down and pet their dogs.

On one occasion, when the libertine faction in Geneva became powerful, the members of that group rallied their forces against those who stood for truth and righteousness and banished John Calvin from their city. The great Reformer's reaction to the bitterness and hatred of his enemies has been preserved for us by his biographers: "Most assuredly if I had merely served man, this would have been poor recompense; but it is my happiness that I have served Him who never fails to reward His servants to the full extent of His promise."[2] Notice especially his words, "who never fails to *reward* His servants to the full extent of His promise."

THE PRINCIPLE OF REWARD

"Reward" differs from "payment" as the apostle Paul makes clear in Romans 4:4. We are remunerated for our services, but a reward is entirely dependent on someone else's kindness toward us. A reward is the result of *grace*.

The Bible teaches that there are degrees of reward, which depend on our faithfulness to God's revealed will. Furthermore, the Lord Jesus often used the promise of future recompense as an incentive to loyal service. And the writer of Hebrews tells us that Moses chose to endure ill-treatment with the people of God rather than enjoy the passing pleasures of sin, *for he was looking to the reward* (Heb. 11:24-26)—God's eternal recompense of his devotion.

The full extent of God's gracious good will toward us is hard to imagine. Paul admitted his inability to describe it when he wrote, "Things which eye has not seen and ear has not heard, and which have not entered the heart of man, all that God has prepared for those who love Him" (1 Cor. 2:9, NASB).

The concept of reward differs in the Old Testament from that of the New, and yet they are connected. In the Old Testament, the blessing of God was both material and spiritual. The condition to be met was a simple one: obedience to His covenant.[3] When the requirement had been met, a threefold blessing would result: (1) continuance as a nation in the land, (2) blessing from God in all areas of life, and (3) anticipation of the fullness of blessing under the reign of the Messiah.

When the Lord Jesus came He offered Himself to Israel as their long-awaited Messiah. Unfortunately for Israel, they rejected Him (cf. Matt. 11:2—12:50). All the material blessings of His Kingdom reign have had to be postponed.[4] We now live in the interim between His two advents.[5] Blessings still accrue to those who obey His revealed will, but the emphasis now is on a *future* reward rather than temporal prosperity (cf. 1 Cor. 9:25; James 1:12; Rev. 2:10).

The essence of this truth was grasped by the German evangelical Bible scholar Bernhard Weiss when he wrote: "As the servants of God in the Israelitish theocracy[6] were entitled, by reason of their covenant relationship, to look for the fulfillment of the promise as the reward for their fulfillment of their covenant obligations, so the disciple of Jesus is entitled to look for the completion of salvation [i.e., his glorification and being forever with the Lord] as the reward for the fulfillment of the demands which are made upon him in virtue of his being a disciple."[7]

Because in this closing section of the book of Ruth we are concerned with Naomi, we will confine ourselves to a consideration of God's recompense to her. The principle not to be overlooked is that *God graciously rewards those who faithfully follow Him and are obedient to His Word.*

A BRIGHTER FUTURE

As we turn to the text we find that Boaz and Ruth have both appeared on the stage for the last time. They now enjoy one of those rare unions in which both husband and wife[8] are selfless and mature, empathetic and understanding, united in their values and goals, and therefore able to grow together personally and spiritually.

As the story began with Naomi, so now it ends with her. The women of the city who had shunned her after her return from Moab now gathered around her and were profuse in their praise. They saw evidence of God's favor toward her and felt that they could now show their approval.

> Blessed [be] *Yahweh*, who has not left you without [lit., caused to fail] a near kinsman;[9] and may his name[10] be called in Israel [i.e., may he become famous]. And may he become to you a restorer of life[11] and a nourisher of your old age; for your daughter-in-law, who loves you[12] and is better to you than seven sons has borne him.
>
> And Naomi took the child and laid him in her bosom,[13] and became his nurse.
>
> And the neighborhood women[14] gave him a name, saying, "A son has been born to Naomi"; and they called his name Obed. He is the father of Jesse, the father of David. [4:14-17]

CHANGE OF FORTUNE

Cox provides a fine connection between the preceding scene and what we find recorded in these verses.

> Boaz, being now the recognised *goel* of Ruth, marries her; and in due time a son is given to them. And now the shadows, which lay so thick on the opening incidents of the Story, clear off, and both Naomi and Ruth receive a full reward for their rare and heroic love. It is one of the many fine points of the Story that its concluding sentences are almost wholly devoted, not to the young and happy wife and mother, but to Naomi, who had suffered so many calamities, and who, by the piety and resignation with which she bore them, had drawn Ruth from the idolatries of Moab. It is Naomi, not Ruth, whom "the women her neighbours" congratulate on the birth of Ruth's son. In him they see Naomi's *goel*—Ruth already had hers in Boaz; and they pray that, as he grows

up, he may restore her to her former happiness and be the stay and gladness of her old age. But though they speak to Naomi, and pray for her, they do not utterly forget the singular virtue of Ruth. In the words, "Thy daughter-in-law, *who loveth thee, who is better to thee than seven sons,*" they pronounce on her an eulogy such as few "strange" women could have heard from Hebrew lips. It is because the boy is Ruth's son that he is Naomi's *goel*; for how can he fail to love and cherish the woman whom his mother has loved with a love even passing that of women?[15]

As we consider more fully what these verses tell us, we cannot help but notice the blessing of God upon Naomi. He has brought the impossible to pass (cf. 1:11-12 with 4:17). She had gone to Moab of her own accord and, following the death of Elimelech, had stayed there of her own free will. Her sons had died in that land, and she had been left with her grief.

With the passing of her loved ones Naomi doubtless felt acute anxiety, for she had been left alone in the world. She may also have felt anger because of the bitterness in her heart toward God and the helplessness of her situation (cf. 1:20-21). And she may also have felt some guilt, for she acknowledged that "the hand of *Yahweh*" had gone out against her (i.e., to chasten her).

Naomi, however, had turned her back on Moab and returned to the place of God's appointment. As one who had repented of a former wrong, she had cast herself upon God and His mercy. Her welcome back to Bethlehem left much to be desired. Her former friends, following their initial greeting, left her strictly alone. "The Lord," they concluded, "was obviously displeased with her; and as evidence of His continued displeasure there is this Moabitess who has accompanied her. The marriages of her sons to foreigners had obviously been the cause of their deaths." And so Naomi was left on her own to cope as best she could.

But Naomi's fortunes had changed, and now those same women spoke glowingly of God's goodness to her. Ruth's newborn son was regarded as Naomi's *gōʾēl* or "redeemer." Certainly Boaz continued in the role of Naomi's supporter, but Obed (who is looked upon as Mahlon's child, cf. 4:10) is to be to her a "restorer of life and a nourisher of her old age."

So it was that God showed special kindness to Naomi. When her sons died in Moab, she had nothing to live for. Hope was gone. Now, however, in honor of her faithfulness to His covenant God had given her a (grand) son. Ruth's child was her reward.

UNNOTICED NO LONGER

Ruth also received the praise of the women of Bethlehem. On the arrival from Moab, Ruth had gone unnoticed. The women came out to greet Naomi, but Ruth was not made welcome. Now they said to Naomi that *Yahweh* had more than compensated her for the loss of Mahlon and Chilion (4:15*b*). Ruth was better than seven sons. Morris comments on their words:

> The love of Ruth for her mother-in-law shines through this book and it is appropriate that it be given this recognition at the end. The tribute, *which is better to thee than seven sons* (*cf.,* I Sam. 1:8), is all the more striking in view of the place usually given boys in comparison with girls. A numerous male progeny was the ambition of all married people and thus to speak of Ruth as being worth more to Naomi than *seven sons* is the supreme tribute. For *seven sons* is proverbial for a perfect family (*cf.,* I Samuel 2:5).[16]

Forgotten now was Ruth's Moabitish ancestry; forgotten too were her years of barrenness, which those who were superstitious may have felt was a punishment from God for some previous sin. Ruth had borne Naomi a son in accordance with the principles of God's covenant. She now received belated but deserved praise.

RITE OF SPRING

With renewed hope in her heart, Naomi took Obed to her heart and showered on him all the love and devotion of a grateful grandmother. She had despaired of ever having grandchildren, and now what was thought to be impossible God had graciously brought to pass.

Something of Naomi's gladness may be realized when we consider that "to Naomi this child was special. She had expected a lonely old age when her husband and sons died. With none of those near to her left her future had indeed looked bleak. But thanks to Ruth's devotion everything was now different. She belonged to a family once more. She was loved and she had a recognized place. The babe in a sense symbolized it all, and Naomi gave herself over to caring for him."[17]

WHAT'S IN A NAME?

Now also the neighbors of Boaz came to rejoice with Naomi. These women gathered about Naomi and gave the young child the name *Obed* (meaning "servant").

We are surprised, however, that Boaz did not name his own son. The closest parallel to this unusual incident is to be found in Luke 1. There, at the birth of the son of Zacharias and Elizabeth, the neighbors and relatives gathered in the home and suggested that the child be named after his father. Only after the protests of his parents was he named John (Luke 1:57-63).

Perhaps because Naomi had no living relatives and because the child was legally reckoned as the son of Mahlon, the women suggested the name Obed. The idea of the lad growing up to serve his grandmother must have struck a responsive chord in their hearts, and so he was called "Servant"—Naomi's helper, the mainstay of her old age.

Further evidence of God's goodness to Naomi may be found in the fact that in time Obed himself would marry. Naomi's great-grandson would be called Jesse, and his son and her great-great-grandson was to be David, Israel's great king.

So God amply rewarded Naomi and fully met all her needs.

LINKED WITH ROYALTY

The mention of Naomi's relationship to David prompted the writer to conclude with a genealogy. The importance to Israelites of those lists of names has been underscored by Marshall D. Johnson. He points out that the genealogies were designed "to establish continuity over those periods of time not covered by material in the tradition."

Having laid down that general principle, Johnson observes that "the *Tôlēdôth* (i.e., genealogy) of Perez appended to the book of Ruth (4:18-22) may similarly be intended to establish continuity during the time of the judges, that is, from the conquest [of the land by Joshua] to the beginning of the Davidic monarchy."[18]

There are some important things to notice in the genealogy, in particular its beginning with Perez the son of Tamar (Gen. 38; Matt. 1:3): "And these [are] the generations of Perez: Perez fathered Hezron, and Hezron fathered Ram, and Ram fathered Amminadab, and Amminadab fathered Nashon, and Nashon fathered Salmon, and Salmon fathered Boaz, and Boaz fathered Obed, and Obed fathered Jesse, and Jesse fathered David" (4:18-22).

THE RECOMPENSE OF REWARD

We should observe from the beginning that this genealogy is probably not complete. Keil and Delitzsch note that Perez's son Hezron was born *before* Jacob went down to Egypt (cf. Gen. 38:29 and 46:12). That took place around 1875 B.C. The exodus from Egypt occurred around 1445 B.C., leaving more than 430 years to be covered from Perez to Nashon. "According to this there are only four or five generations to the 430 years spent by the Israelites in Egypt."[19]

These scholars continue: "The omission of unimportant members becomes still more apparent in the statement which follows, *viz.*, that Nashon begat *Salmah* [Salmon], and Salmah, *Boaz,* in which only two generations are given for a space of more than 250 years."[20]

Such facts should not disturb us, for it is evident from other genealogies that the lists in the Bible are representative.[21]

A second point of emphasis in the genealogy is the appearance of Boaz's name. Obed was regarded as the son of Mahlon, not Boaz, so the mention of Boaz is somewhat surprising.

One explanation is that it seems as if the blessing pronounced on Boaz was borne out in the history of events. Mahlon seems to have been bypassed in David's ancestral record in favor of Boaz.

Morris says that "Obed [in this genealogy] is treated simply as the son of Boaz. In a sense he carried on Mahlon's name and succeeded to his property. But in an official genealogy he is treated as the son of his true father."[22]

However true that might be, may we not be overlooking God's gracious recompense of *Boaz* by linking him with David? It seems preferable to include the idea that the writer, under the gentle leading of the Holy Spirit, has artlessly shown God's favor to Boaz as well as Naomi.

A final observation concerns Ruth. Her name appears in the genealogy of Christ (Matt. 1:5). There she is linked with Tamar and Rahab. That is most unusual, for women were not normally included in such records. Charles H. Spurgeon, the famous British expositor of the nineteenth century, commented on the inclusion of Ruth in the ancestral line of the Lord Jesus: "We note that . . . Gentile blood mingled with the Hebrew strain. Our King [Christ] . . . is heir of a line in which flows the blood of . . . the rustic Ruth; he is akin to the fallen and the lowly, and he will show his love even to the poorest and the most obscure."[23] In His birth Jesus demonstrated His grace toward us by being identified with our humanity.

MORE THAN AN APPENDIX

But some will ask, Why did the writer end his story with a list of names? Isn't that a strange way to conclude a book? What does God intend us to learn from those verses?

The author does not tell us why he finished his book that way. The concluding paragraphs, however, emphasize God's grace to Ruth in her marriage to Boaz, and His favor also to Naomi. It seems, therefore, as if the verses that end the story should in some way continue that theme.

As we look back to Perez and forward to David, we are given cause to see how God's lovingkindness to Boaz and Ruth far exceeded anything they could have expected. He made them part of a line that led up to the great King David,[24] "a man after the heart of God" (Acts 13:22), and forever enshrined their names in the ancestry of Him who is King of kings and Lord of lords.

Furthermore, this brief genealogy, became part of one record (1 Chron. 2:3ff.) and then another (Matt. 1), so that we begin to glimpse God's masterful, overarching plan for our redemption. His hand controls history; He works out His purpose in the lives of His people from one generation to the next; His plan has continuity and purpose. We may see only a little of it, and our understanding of His ways may be obscured by limitations imposed by the Fall, but these concluding verses remind us that He is over all His works. His plan cannot be thwarted—He elects to positions of honor whomsoever He will. And while we are subject to all the limitations of the flesh, He continues to deal with us in grace and offer us the promise of a future recompense if we will but obey Him. His dealings with Naomi and Ruth furnish ample proof of His kind intent toward the lowliest of His followers!

Notes

Introduction

1. Cf. J. Lilley, "Ruth," *ZPEB*, 5:176.
2. Cf. Harrison, p. 1059.
3. Hermann Gunkel, *Die Religion in Geschichte und Gegenwart* (Göttingen: Vandenhoeck and Ruprecht, 1916), 4, col. 2181, and Robert H. Pfeiffer, *Introduction to the Old Testament* (New York: Harper and Brothers, 1941), p. 718, both deny that the events of the book of Ruth are historical. H. H. Rowley, however, in *Growth of the Old Testament* (London: Hutchinson's U. Library, 1950), p. 150, accepts the historicity of the events even though he does not believe the book was written until the postexilic period.
4. Although the Talmud did not come into existence until the Tannaic period (A.D. 200-500), it did serve as a "hedge" about the sacred writings of the Jews and sought to preserve their ancient heritage—a heritage that some Jews claim was current as far back as the eighth century B.C. (see Josephus *Antiquities of the Jews* XIII. 297). Baba Bathra 14b reads: "Samuel wrote the book which bears his name and the Book [note the use of the singular] of Judges and Ruth" (*Babylonian Talmud*, XI:71).
5. KD, 4:466.
6. Higher biblical criticism has assigned the writing of the book of Deuteronomy to the reign of Josiah (622 B.C.). Not prepared to yield their presupposition to contrary evidence, those who espouse a late date for Deuteronomy feel compelled to date the book of Ruth (1) after the time of Josiah, (2) during the Babylonian exile, or (3) in the postexilic period of Ezra-Nehemiah, for the contents of Ruth give evidence of a knowledge of Deuteronomy. For a competent discussion of the dating of Deuteronomy see Archer, pp. 251-62.
7. Certain words (supposedly of Aramaic origin or characteristic of later Hebrew) are frequently cited as proof of the late date of Ruth: e.g., *nāśā nāšîm*, "they took wives" (1:4); *lāhēn*, "for them" (1:13); *ʿāgan*, "endure" (1:13); *mārā*ʾ, "bitter" (1:20); *ʿānâ be*, "has eyed me" (1:21); *miqreh*, "chance" (2:3); *ta ʿabûrî*, "leave" (2:8); *yiqṣōrûn*, "harvest" (2:9); *tidbāqîn*, "stay close" (2:21); *yāradty*, "go down" (3:3); *šākābty*, "lie down" (3:4); *ta ʿaśîn*, "to do" (3:4); *margēlōt*, "feet(?)" (3:7, 8, 14); *tēdeʿîn*, "shall know"

135

(3:18); *pelōnî ʾalmōnî,* "such a one(?)" (4:1); *qayyēm,* "confirm" (4:7); and *šālap na ʿalô,* "draw off . . . his sandal" (4:7). See L. P. Smith, "The Book of Ruth," *Interpreter's Bible* (Nashville: Abingdon, 1956), 2:830. Morris, however, quotes D. J. Wiseman of the British Museum as affirming that these words "are now known from the Middle Babylonian and Middle Assyrian period, c. 1400 B.C.!" (p. 233).

8. See C. F. Keil, *Lehrbuch der historisch-kritischen Einleitung in die Schriften des Alten Testaments* (Leipzig: J. C. Mohr, 1873), p. 437. Harrison says, "The direct character of the narrative seems to imply that David had not yet become the legendary personage of Israel" (p. 1061). With this E. J. Young, *An Introduction to the Old Testament* (Grand Rapids: Eerdmans, 1949), p. 330, is in essential agreement.

9. These include (roughly in accordance with the date assigned the book by each writer) Wright, p. xliv, with which compare his later *Introduction to the Old Testament* (New York: T. Whitaker, 1890), p. 126; Driver, pp. 454ff.; Hertzberg, p. 257; Rudolph, p. 29; F. W. Albright, "Ruth," in H. C. Alleman and E. E. Flack, *Old Testament Commentary* (Philadelphia: Fortress, 1954), p. 147; R. Hals, *The Theology of the Book of Ruth* (Philadelphia: Fortress, 1969), p. 73; G. von Rad, *Old Testament Theology* (Philadelphia: Westminster, 1962), 1:52; W. W. Cannon, "The Book of Ruth," *Theology* 16 (1928), p. 315; and S. Davidson, *Introduction to the Old Testament* (Edinburgh: T. & T. Clark, 1862), 1:482ff.

10. G. H. A. von Ewald, *Geschichte des Volkes Israel* (Göttingen: Dietericht, 1864), p. 225; E. König, *Einleitung in das Alte Testament* (Leipzig: J. C. Hinrichs, 1893), p. 287; Sasson, p. 244.

11. Cf. O. Eissfeldt, *The Old Testament: An Introduction* (Philadelphia: Westminster, 1965), p. 483; G. Fohrer, *Introduction to the Old Testament* (London: S. P. C. K., 1970), pp. 251-52; Gray, p. 398-400; Joüon, *Ruth,* pp. 12ff.; W. O. E. Oesterley and T. H. Robinson, *Introduction to the Books of the Old Testament* (Oxford: Clarendon, 1950), p. 150; D. R. Ap-Thomas, "The Book of Ruth," *ET* 79 (1968), pp. 369-73. See also B. S. Childs, *Introduction to the Old Testament as Scripture* (Philadelphia: Fortress, 1979), where he makes a claim that the writer of Ruth "drew material from I Chronicles 2 in order to confirm the testimony" (p. 567). However, might not the writer of Chronicles have taken his material from the book of Ruth?

12. C. Cornhill, *Introduction to the Canonical Books of the Old Testament* (New York: G. P. Putnam's Sons, 1907), p. 255.

13. Myers, p. 19ff. The archaic forms are thought to be: *tidbāqîn,* "stay" (2:8, 21); *yiqṣōrûn,* "harvest" (2:9); *yišʾ abûn,* "draw" (2:9); *weyāradty,* "and go down" (3:3); *wešākābty,* "and lie down" (3:4); *ta ʿasîn,* "you are to do" (3:4); *tede ʿîn,* "you shall know" (3:18); *qāniṯāy,* "you buy, acquire" (4:5). Myers, however, does not believe that Ruth went through a twofold form of transmission. See also G. Glanzman, "The Origin and Date of the Book of Ruth," *CBQ* 21 (1959), pp. 201-7, and M. Crook, "The Book of Ruth," *JBL* 16 (1948), pp. 155f.

14. Gerleman, 18:7-8.

15. J. J. Davis, *Conquest and Crisis* (Grand Rapids: Baker, 1969), p. 156, and L. J. Wood, *Distressing Days of the Judges* (Grand Rapids: Zondervan, 1975), p. 254.

16. S. M. Zwemer, *Sons of Adam* (Grand Rapids: Baker, 1951), p. 17. See also J. Coppens, *The Old Testament and Its Critics*, trans. by E. A. Ryan and E. W. Tribbe (Patterson, N.J.: St. Anthony Guild Press, 1942), p. 75.

17. W. S. Churchill, "Moses: The Leader of a People," *Sunday Chronicle*, 8 November 1931, p. 7.

18. Cornill (pp. 464f.) believes that *kanōn* was a "Semitic loan-word" that the early Greeks adopted and adapted. He cites illustrations from Greek literature that he believes show that *kanōn* originally meant "wood" (similar to the Semitic *kaneh*, "reed." See Homer *The Iliad*, 8.193, 13.407, and 23.761). He then refers his readers to the usage of the word in Ezekiel 40:3 where it had come to mean "the rule of the carpenter." In later Greek *kanōn* acquired the sense of "norm, rule, standard."

19. *Mishnah*, Yadim, 3:2; 4:5 (see H. Danby's translation, pp. 781, 784).

20. Flavius Josephus, "Contra Apion," *The Works of Josephus* (1926), 1:8.

21. See P. Katz, *Zeitschrift für die Neutestamentliche Wissenschaft*, 47 (1956), pp. 199-201.

22. See the writings of the brilliant Semitic scholar, R. Laird Harris, in *Inspiration and Canonicity of the Bible* (Chicago: Moody, 1957); "Was the Law and the Prophets Two Thirds of the Canon?" *Bulletin of the Evangelical Theological Society*, 9 (1966), pp. 163-71; and "Canon," *ZPEB*, 1:709-31 in which he argues persuasively for a twofold division of the Old Testament.

23. Cf. H. B. Swete, *An Introduction to the Old Testament in Greek* (New York: Ktav, 1968), pp. 197-264.

24. According to W. Smith and H. Wace, *A Dictionary of Christian Biography* (London: John Murray, 1882), "Melito, bishop of Sardis, the capital of Lydia, held, in the third quarter of the 2nd century, a foremost place among the bishops of Asia, both in respect of personal influence and literary activity" (4:894). Eusebius of Pamphylia, in his *Historia Ecclesiasticus*, quotes from a letter written by Melito in which he refers to a visit to Palestine where he diligently ascertained "the accurate facts about their writings, how many they are in number, and what is their order" (iv. 26. 13f.). In the list provided by Melito, Ruth comes immediately after Judges.

25. J. P. Audet, "A Hebrew-Aramaic List of Books of the Old Testament in Greek Transcription," *JTS*, New Series, 1 (1950), pp. 135-54.

26. The "Writings" or *Hagiographa* included Psalms, Proverbs, Job, Daniel, Ezra-Nehemiah (counted as one book), 1 and 2 Chronicles (also counted as one book), and the five *Megilloth* or rolls used at separate festivals (Song of Solomon at Passover; Ruth at the Feast of Weeks; Lamentations on the ninth of Ab, the day of the destruction of the Temple; Ecclesiastes at the Feast of Tabernacles; and Esther at Purim). See also W. W. Cannon, "The Book of Ruth," *Theology* 16 (1928), p. 317.

27. This is the reason Bewer (p. 428) gives for the exclusion of Daniel from the prophetic writings.

28. According to Cornill (pp. 472-80) and Eissfeldt (pp. 565-68) the Pentateuch was written between 950-450 B.C. Because of its notable place in the history of God's ancient people, this portion of the canon was quickly closed. The Prophets, however, took longer to be recognized as authoritative and that portion of the canon did not close until 200 B.C. The third stage, the canonization of the Writings, did not come until A.D. 90 when, following the destruction of the Temple and the dispersion of the Jews, some authoritative record of those writings they held sacred was at last made. See A. Spanier's article "Canon," *Universal Jewish Encyclopedia* (New York: Universal Jewish Encyclopedia, 1941), 3:12. We find such theories untenable.

29. J. P. Lewis, "What Do We Mean by Jamnia?" *JBR* 32 (1964), pp. 125-32.

30. *Introductory Guide to the Old Testament* (Grand Rapids: Zondervan, 1951), pp. 126-27. See also Harrison, p. 278, and Archer, pp. 66-72.

31. W. E. Staples, "The Book of Ruth," *AJSL* 53 (1937), pp. 145ff.; L. P. Smith, *Interpreter's Bible*, 2:830; H. May, "Ruth's Visit to the High Place at Bethlehem," *JRAS* 75 (1939), pp. 75-78; and S. Shearman and J. Curtis, "Divine-Human Conflicts in the Old Testament," *JNES* 28 (1969), pp. 235-40. Eissfeld says: "Staples' view that all the names which appear in the book have reference to the fertility cult is no more probable than his assertion that the book, which in his view reveals many other motifs belonging to this cult, is intended to depict the transition from sorrow to joy in the course of the world's life, and to present the birth of a child as the sign of a more fortunate age" (p. 481).

32. "The Theme of the Ruth Story," *CBQ* 22 (1960), p. 391.

33. R. G. Moulton, *The Modern Reader's Bible* (New York: Macmillan, 1937), pp. 1375-76. See also W. McKane, *Tracts for the Times: Ruth, Esther, Lamentations, Ecclesiastes, Song of Songs* (London: SCM, 1965), p. 12; S. Bertram, "Symmetrical Design in the Book of Ruth," *JBL* 84 (1965), pp. 165-68; and D. Rauber, "Literary Values in Ruth," *JBL* 89 (1970), pp. 27-37.

34. Sasson, p. 197. In *Archaeology and the Religion of Israel* (1950), W. F. Albright, however, pointed out that "the Israelites had developed a previously unknown type of narrative style, simple and direct, equally suited for recounting tales and for recounting historical episodes. . . . The delicacy of the story of Ruth remains unsurpassed anywhere; Ruth's loyalty to her mother-in-law, the scene between her and Boaz in chapter three, and the final episode with Naomi (4:14-17) are gems of world literature" (*Archaeology and the Religion of Israel* [Baltimore: Johns Hopkins U., 1953], pp. 22-23).

35. Driver, p. 456.

36. Eissfeldt, pp. 480ff.; and a reply, "The Plot of the Book of Ruth," *BJRL* 32 (1950), pp. 207-28.

37. J. Titterington, "A Case Study in Friendship," *His* (Jan. 1976), pp. 1, 4ff.;

Interpreter's Bible (Nashville: Abingdon), 2:831; R. G. Moulton, *Biblical Idyls* (Boston: D. C. Heath, 1896), p. xxvi.

38. J. Hempel, *Das Ethos des Alten Testaments* (Berlin: A. Töpelmann, 1938), p. 172.
39. I. Bettan, *The Five Scrolls* (Cincinnati: Union of American Hebrew Congregations), p. 53.
40. L. Ryken, *The Literature of the Bible* (Grand Rapids: Zondervan, 1974), p. 72.
41. KD, 4:466.
42. G. Campbell Morgan, *Living Messages of the Books of the Bible* (Old Tappan, N.J.: Revell, 1912), pp. 134-36.
43. Ibid., pp. 136-37.
44. KD, 4:466.
45. Fuerst, p. 5; cf. also Eissfeldt, p. 479; E. Selin, *Introduction to the Old Testament,* p. 250; Driver, pp. 455f.; W. R. Smith, "The Book of Ruth," *Encyclopedia Biblica* (London: A. and C. Black, 1907), 4:col. 4169; P. Joüon, *Ruth,* p. 96; and many others.
46. A. Jepsen, "Das Buch Ruth," *Theologische Studien und Kritiken* 108 (1937-1938), pp. 416-28, believes that the book was written during the exilic period. He says: "And when it is now recorded how contrary to despair and despondency, a new heir is presented to Naomi, this was for the exiled in their despondency a word which comforted them and filled them with new courage. So it cannot be denied that the book of Ruth with this interpretation is understandable especially in the time of the exile.

    "Israel had, as the childless barren widow, as the deserted wife, nothing to expect from the future, just like the widow Naomi, who was robbed of her children."
47. R. Hals, *The Theology of the Book of Ruth* (1969), p. 75. By way of contrast, Sasson (p. 232) believes that the book was written at a time when the Davidic dynasty was almost extinct. Its composition was intended to bolster David's claim to the throne.
48. See C. J. Barber, *Nehemiah and the Dynamics of Effective Leadership* (Neptune, N.J.: Loizeaux, 1976), pp. 121-47. Not to be overlooked in this discussion is the spiritual awakening of chaps. 8-10 and the signing of a covenant by the people pledging their loyalty to the Word of the Lord. See also W. R. Eichhorst, "Ezra's Ethics on Intermarriage and Divorce," *Grace Journal* 10 (Fall 1969), pp. 16-28.
49. Those favoring the view that Ruth is a polemic against Ezra and Nehemiah include R. H. Pfeiffer, *Introduction to the Old Testament,* pp. 717ff., and G. A. F. Knight, *Ruth and Jonah,* pp. 15-23.
50. Margaret B. Crook, "The Book of Ruth," *JBR* 16 (1948), pp. 155-60.
51. S. Davidson, 1:482ff.; cf. Wright, *Introduction to the Old Testament,* p. 126; Young, p. 339.
52. B. Vellas, "The Book of Ruth and Its Purpose" *Theologia Athens* XXV (1954), pp. 7ff. See also G. A. Cooke, *The Book of Ruth* (Cambridge:

Cambridge U., 1918), p. xiii; Hertzberg, p. 258; H. H. Rowley, *Growth of the Old Testament,* p. 151; and "The Marriage of Ruth," *HTR* 40 (1947), p. 78.

53. L. Finkelstein, *The Pharisees* (New York: Ktav, 1938), 2:540. See also the *Talmud,* Yebamoth, 47b; *Middrash Rabbah,* Ruth 2:22-24.

54. D. Harvey, "Ruth, Book of," *Interpreter's Dictionary of the Bible,* 4:133.

55. Vellas, pp. 10ff. See also H. Bronkers, "Enkele Opmerkingen over Het Verband Tussen Lessing en Leviraat in Ruth IV," *Nederlands Theologisch Tijdschrift* 2 (1947-48), pp. 2-7.

56. H. P. Hyatt, "Ruth, Book of," *HDB* (1963), p. 865. Bronkers, cited above, says: "A careful study of the content of this chapter can lead to no other conclusion than that the author here attempts to make acceptable that under certain circumstances the concept of redemption ought to include the obligation to levirate marriage even in its most extensive form. An extension of the obligation to redeem is propagated here, an extension which according to the author always existed in earlier times but which in his day had fallen into disuse" (p. 4). See also, E. Neufeld, *The Hittite Laws* (London: Luzac and Co., 1951), p. 192, and G. R. Driver and J. C. Miles, *The Assyrian Laws* (Oxford: Clarendon, 1935), p. 242. These all support, on philological and historical grounds, a widening of the levirate marriage custom.

57. Rowley, "The Marriage of Ruth," *HTR* 40 (1947), p. 171. See also M. Burrows, "Levirate Marriage in Israel," *JBL* 59 (1940), pp. 23-33; "The Ancient Oriental Background of Hebrew Levirate Marriage," *BASOR* 77 (1940), pp. 2-15; and E. Neufeld, *Ancient Hebrew Marriage Laws* (London: Longmans, Green, 1944), pp. 23-55.

58. S. R. Driver, *Critical and Exegetical Commentary on Deuteronomy* (Edinburgh: T. & T. Clark, 1896), p. 285. Cf. L. M. Epstein's claim that a sharp distinction exists between levirate and * geʾ ullah* marriage, in *Marriage Laws in the Bible and the Talmud* (Cambridge, Mass.: Harvard U., 1942), pp. 86-89. That distinction is held by many competent scholars.

59. This concept is fleshed out by D. F. Rauber, "Literary Values in the Bible; The Book of Ruth," *JBL* 89 (1970), pp. 27-37.

60. O. Loretz, "The Theme of the Ruth Story," *CBQ* 22 (1960), pp. 391-99.

61. *Das Buch Ruth,* p. 32.

62. *Ruth,* p. 242.

63. Rudolph says, "Certainly the narrator exercises all care in the portrayal of the individual characters . . . That Ruth arrives at the right field, however, is Yahweh's leading; that the clever plan of Naomi comes to fruition is Yahweh's mercy and that the desired son is produced from the marriage with Boaz is Yahweh's gift" (p. 32).

64. A. Jepsen, "Das Buch Ruth," *Theologische Studien und Kritiken* 108 (1937-38), p. 423.

65. *Ruth,* p. 242.

66. KD, 4:466.

Chapter 1

1. *The Thurber Carnival* (New York: Modern Library, 1957), pp. 47-51.
2. This *waw* consecutive is frequently translated "now." Because here it is connected to the imperfect, some Bible scholars have assumed that the book of Ruth was originally part of another work. This construction is also found at the beginning of Leviticus, Numbers, Joshua, Judges, 1 Samuel, 2 Kings, 2 Chronicles, Nehemiah, Esther, and Ezekiel.
3. "Bethlehem-judah" is a specific term used by the historian to distinguish this small Judean town from the larger and better known (at that time) city in Zebulun (Josh. 19:15; see also Mic. 5:2 [Heb. 5:1]).
4. A large number of expositors believe the famine of Ruth 1 is to be dated at the time of the Midianite and Amalekite invasion when these peoples came up "as grasshoppers for multitude, to destroy the land" (see Judg. 6).
5. The scene is described eloquently by Cox, pp. 44-48.
6. The writer specifically uses the term "the fields of Moab" (1:1-2, 6). Had he so desired, he could have employed the word ʾerets, "land" (cf. 1:7 where ʾerets is used to describe "the land of Judah"). His emphasis of the "fields," therefore, is deemed to be intentional.
7. See Morris, pp. 249f.; Cox, p. 45.
8. In antiquity, Hebrew names often reflected the religious connections of one's parents or were given to a child because the parents discerned a characteristic in their son or daughter that brought some name to mind. Recent studies have shown that names ending in *melek* were invariably held by people of noble descent. The names Mahlon and Chilion occur in literature outside the Bible. The reason these names were given, and their significance, is still a matter of conjecture. See Sasson, pp. 18f. The explanation of W. E. Staples, "The Book of Ruth," *AJSL* 53 (1937), pp. 145-57, that the names of all the family members indicate a connection with the fertility cult lacks credibility.
9. The change in the verb from *gûr*, "to sojourn (as an alien)" to *wayyihû*, "to remain there" is therefore most significant. (In v. 3 further regression is evident. Following the death of Elimelech, the sons settled [*wayyēsebû*, "to dwell"] in Moab. The ten years they spent in Moab proved they had no thought of returning to Judah.)
10. Psychologists have discerned that for a person to feel secure enough to settle in a given place he or she needs to experience a sense of belongingness, worth, and competence. See the excellent articles by Gary H. Strauss, "What Really Happened in Eden?" *Psychology for Living* (Dec. 1976), pp. 18-19; (Jan. 1977), pp. 16-17; and (Feb. 1977), pp. 16-17. Elimelech and Naomi must have both experienced this, for he decided "to remain" in Moab (changing his earlier plan), and she even decided to remain in this foreign land after her husband had died.
11. Cox, p. 53.
12. Fuller, p. 23.

13. The Hebrew construction of 1:3 is unusual. See Morris, p. 250.
14. The *Midrash* makes Ruth the daughter of Eglon, king of Moab. This claim is without substance. It has been accepted, however, by Geoffrey T. Bull, *Love Song in Harvest* (London: Pickering & Inglis, 1972), pp. 18ff.
15. Morris (pp. 250-51) has some sage comments on the meanings of these names.
16. *Talmud*, Baba Bathra, 91a.
17. Cf. God's dealings with Jonah in C. J. Barber and G. H. Strauss, *The Effective Parent* (San Bernardino, Calif.: Here's Life, 1980), pp. 3-81.
18. Cf. Deuteronomy 1:8; 3:20; 4:5, 14; 5:31; 6:1, 10, 18, 23; 7:13; 8:1; 9:5; 10:11; 11:9-12, 21; 12:1; 15:4; 19:2, 8, 14; 25:19; 26:3. See P. D. Miller, Jr., "The Gift of God," *Interpretation* 28 (1969): 451-65.
19. See R. Morosco, "Theological Implications of Fear," *Journal of Psychology and Theology* 1, 2 (1973): 43-50.
20. These criteria are based on Paul's distinctions in 1 Corinthians 8:1—11:1. They may be studied in Charles R. Erdman's delightful little commentary *The First Epistle to the Corinthians* (Philadelphia: Westminster, 1927), pp. 75-96.

Chapter 2

1. C. J. Barber, *Vital Encounter* (San Bernardino, Calif.: Here's Life, 1979), pp. 123-32.
2. This definition has been adapted from John R. W. Stott's handling of *agapē* love in *The Epistles of John* (Grand Rapids: Eerdmans, 1964). 230 pp.
3. Cf. Deuteronomy 14:29; 16:11; 24:19; 26:12; Psalm 94:6 for special legislation designed to alleviate some of their distress. God made Himself the protector of widows (Ps. 68:5) and executed justice on their behalf (Deut. 10:18; 27:19). His beneficent laws, however, were flouted (Ps. 94:6; Isa. 1:23; Mal. 3:5).
4. Morris has observed, "When God visits, everything depends on the state of affairs He finds. The verb is a warning against presuming on the holiness of God and a reminder that God delights to bless. On this occasion His visit means the end of famine. The bread now available is regarded as God's gift" (p. 252).
5. The question is naturally raised, Why should each return to the house of her *mother*? Were their fathers dead? Ruth 2:11 seems to imply that Ruth's father still was alive. Keil and Delitzsch conjecture that their mothers would know how to comfort them. Others believe that in this verse we have evidence of a matriarchal system (see D. R. Mace, *Hebrew Marriage* [London: Hutchinson's U. Library, 1953], pp. 81ff.). Campbell provides a list of the reasons given by others why the young widows should return to their mothers' houses and concludes that, based upon evidence gleaned from Genesis 24 and the Song of Solomon (3:4; 8:2), "The 'mother's house' was the focus for matters pertinent to marriage, especially for discussion and planning for marriage" (p. 64). To this discussion should be added the weight of Morris's research

and reflection. "In a polygamous society the place for such as Ruth and Orpah would be the women's quarters presided over by the mother" (p. 253).

6. For a discussion of *ḥēsēd* see *TWOT*, 1:698-700; N. Glueck, *Hesed in the Bible* (Leiden: E. J. Brill, 1967); K. Sakenfeld, *The Meaning of Hesed in the Bible* (Missoula, Mont.: Scholars Press, 1978).

7. "With you," *ʿimmākem*, is masculine, whereas we would have expected a feminine form. It is the first of seven instances in which a masculine plural occurs with a feminine antecedent. (The second is "you have done" in this verse; then "to you," 1:9, 11; "than for you," 1:13; and "the two of them" 1:19*b*; 4:11). Joüon, *Grammaire*, (#149b [pp. 457-58]) believes that these masculine forms are evidence of a late date of composition for the book of Ruth. Myers (p. 20) has refuted this theory. Campbell (p. 65) concludes his review of the discussion by offering his own theory that this was an *early* Hebrew feminine dual suffix that ended in *-m*, just as the masculine plural ending does, but contrasted with the feminine plural *-n*. One exception to this theory occurs in verse 19. A possible explanation is that this masculine usage may be a way of referring to corporate personality and be an evidence of *early* Hebrew philological history. See also Morris, p. 255f.

8. For a discussion of *menûḥah*, "rest," see *TWOT*, 2:1323f.

9. Cox, pp. 65-67.

10. See Joüon, *Ruth*, p. 36; Morris, p. 254.

11. The usage of *kî*, here translated "No," has been challenged by some lexicographers and grammarians (see Köehler and Baumgartner's *Lexicon in Veteris Testamentum libros* [Leiden: E. J. Brill, 1951-1953], pp. 431-33; Joüon, *Ruth*, pp. 40-41). However, C. Brockelmann, *Hebräische Syntax* Neukirchen, Kreis Moers: Verlag der Buchhandlung des Erzeinhung svereins, 1956), #134a, and Kennedy, p. 16, are quite prepared to accept its adversative usage.

12. Naomi could obviously marry again. What she is alluding to here is her inability to bear children. See Morris, p. 257.

13. Campbell (p. 67) neatly identifies the three parts to the protasas of Naomi's statement and then explains the apodosis.

14. The *halāhēn* of verse 13, "for them," has been widely regarded as an Aramaism and ipso facto evidence of the late date for the writing of Ruth. The pendulum of modern scholarly opinion is now swinging in the opposite direction and many are seeing the usage of this word as further evidence for the early composition of the book. Cf. Campbell, p. 68; Morris, p. 257. However, amending the text to *lāhēn* as some textual critics do is to resort to a highly questionable expedient.

15. Reference here is obviously to the practice of levirate marriage (Deut. 25:5-10). Cf., Leggett; H. H. Rowley, "The Marriage of Ruth," *HTR* 4 (1947), pp. 77-99 ; M. Burrows, "The Ancient Oriental Background of Levirate Marriage," *BASOR* 70 (1940), pp. 2-15; Mace, pp. 95-118; Neufeld, *Ancient Hebrew Marriage Laws* (1944), pp. 23-55; T. and D.

Thompson, "Some Legal Problems in the Book of Ruth," *VT* 28 (1968), pp. 79-99; de Vaux, *Ancient Israel*, pp. 24-38, 521f.

16. See Gray, p. 410; *TWOT*, 1:132; J. J. M. Roberts, "The Hand of Yahweh," *VT* (1971), pp. 244-51.

17. Watson, p. 376; see also George Lawson, *Exposition of the Book of Ruth* (Edinburgh: J. Ritchie, 1805), pp. 35ff.

18. Cox, pp. 68-70.

19. Campbell, p. 72. A "one-way" kiss of farewell is usual in stories of the conclusion of a relationship.

20. Watson, p. 376.

21. It has been conjectured that this oath was probably accompanied by some expressive gesture such as simulating one's throat being cut by passing a finger across it. The formula for the oath Ruth used is found only here and in 1 Samuel 3:17; 14:44; 20:13; 25:22; 1 Kings 2:23; 20:10; 2 Kings 6:31.

22. Morris says: "As Ruth was much younger than Naomi and would probably live longer this implies that she will so identify herself with Naomi's community that she will stay on there after Naomi's death. The reference to burial seems scarcely to be needed, but we must bear in mind that for the ancient world proper burial was of great importance. . . . We should not overlook [Ruth's] use of the divine name 'Yahweh.' She does not invoke Chemosh or the gods generally. She has taken Yahweh to be her God and it is upon Him accordingly that she calls" (p. 261). See also Wright, p. 17.

23. Taylor (p. 23) reminds us of Thomas Arnold, the great British educator, who first won the hearts of the young boys of Rugby College to himself and then, when they had learned that they could trust him, he pointed them to the Savior (see A. P. Stanley's *Life and Correspondence of Thomas Arnold* [Boston: Fields, Osgood, n.d.]).

24. Watson, p. 379.

25. See Morris's "Additional Note," pp. 264-68.

26. The word order in the original shows the emphasis of Naomi's words. It may be rendered, "Full I went out, and empty [*Yahweh*] has brought me back." Naomi's "I" stands first in the sentence and *Yahweh* last, showing the polarization Naomi felt.

27. The feminine form of "and *they* said" shows that it was the women who were in the city and came out to greet Naomi. See KD, 4:476.

28. The Niphal of the root *hwm* gives evidence of the excitement of those in Bethlehem on recognizing Naomi (cf. 1 Sam. 4:5 and 1 Kings 1:45, where the same word is used). The delight of the women found no response in Naomi's heart. She was still mourning the loss of her loved ones.

29. Morris (pp. 264-68) has a good discussion of the meaning of *Shaddai*.

30. Taylor, pp. 25-26.

Chapter 3

1. Howard J. Ruff, *How to Prosper in the Coming Bad Years* (San Ramon, Calif.: Target, 1979), pp. 3-5.

2. Naomi alludes to this in verse 20, "Call me not Naomi . . . for the Almighty has dealt very bitterly with me . . . the LORD has testified against me and the Almighty has afflicted me." Later, the rabbis coined a saying, "Whom the Lord loveth He maketh rich."

3. *Meyuddāᶜ*, the Pual participle of *ydᶜ*, "to know," refers in this context to a blood relative, acquaintance, or kinsman; someone from the same tribe, but not a brother. Campbell (pp. 88-90) proposes changing the root *myd* to *mwd*, "covenant-brother," but he has been answered by Sasson (p. 39). Morris (p. 268) prefers the term "kinsman."

   Those who see in the biblical writer's use of this word a "deliberate archaism" should reconsider the case for the true antiquity of the book of Ruth. Driver has pointed out that "the general Hebrew style (the idioms and syntax) shows no marks of deterioration . . . and stands on a level with the best parts of Samuel" (p. 454).

4. *Mimmišpaḥat*, "of the family of," has posed problems for translators. Joüon, *Ruth* (p. 46), is of the opinion that the preposition should be translated "by," and that *mišpāḥāh* be given the force of "by the husband." But *mišpāḥāh* is regularly and consistently used of a subdivision of a tribe (e.g., "clan" or part of an extended family). See F. I. Andersen, "Israelite Kinship Terminology and Social Structure," *BT* 20 (1969), pp. 29-39, and deVaux, pp. 4-13.

5. See KD, "According to rabbinic tradition, which is not well established however, Boaz was the nephew of Elimelech" (4:477).

6. The term *ᵓîš gibbôr ḥayil*, "a mighty man of valor," may best be likened to a medieval knight. He was a man who had proved his worth on the field of battle and, in the course of time, had accumulated a measure of wealth. Morris only partly agrees with this conclusion. He writes, "[The term] applied originally to a man distinguished for military prowess, but it is now used widely of those whose excellence lies in other fields. In the Old Testament it most often has to do with fighting capacity. Boaz may have been a warrior, for these were troubled times and any man might have to fight. But in this book he appears rather as a solid citizen." (p. 269). See *TDOT*, 2:373-77.

7. See Judges 6:12; 11:1; 1 Samuel 9:1; 1 Kings 11:28; 2 Kings 15:20, where *gibbôrē ḥāyil* is used.

8. Ruth's ethnic origin is kept constantly before the reader. That is not without significance, and the word "Moabitess" is accompanied by the article in five specific instances (1:22, 2:2, 21; 4:5, 10). The vulnerability of Ruth's situation is stressed in this chapter.

9. This word is in the singular. Taylor writes, "The field to which Ruth went, though apparently one large and undivided area, was really made up of the aggregate portions of land possessed by those who dwelt in Bethlehem. Just as, even at the present day, in some parts of Switzerland, the agricultural population live in villages round which their several patches of land lie—not

cut up by hedges or fenced off by stone walls—but forming what appears to be one immense field, though it is actually very carefully mapped out and divided by landmarks which are perfectly recognizable by the inhabitants themselves; so it was, long ago, in Bethlehem. To a casual visitor there would seem to be but one field, but yet the portion of each proprietor was marked sometimes by heaps of small stones, and sometimes by single upright stones placed at short but regular intervals from each other. This enables us to understand the precept against the removal of a neighbor's landmark, and explains why in the narrative before us the word 'field' is in the singular, and why it is said that Ruth found her place of privilege in the 'part of the field which belonged to Boaz.'"

10. *᾽Aḥar ᾽ašer ᾽emṣā᾽-ḥēn be ῾ēnāyw,* "after him in whose eyes I shall find favor," has been variously interpreted. Campbell reminds us that this was a frequently used idiom that "seems always to be used by a person of inferior status to a superior" (p. 92). The law, however, specifically stated that widows and foreigners were to be allowed to glean (Lev. 19:9f.; 23:22; Deut. 24:19) for, as Morris observes, "Gleaning was not dependent upon the whim of land-owners" (p. 270). Ruth's discretion is seen in her willingness to persevere until she found a friendly landowner (someone who would look on her with favor).

11. This is a unique expression found only here and in Ecclesiastes 2:14-15.

12. See also C. Ellison, *Loneliness* (Chappaqua, N.Y.: Christian Herald, 1980), and H. C. Warlick's *Conquering Loneliness* (Waco, Tex.: Word, 1979).

13. See B. M. Newman and P. R. Newman, *Development Through Life,* (Homewood, Ill.: Dorsey Press, 1975). I have added the element of *hope* for biblical reasons. Some psychologists may call this actualization or assign it a term involving the concept of a future-orientation. It seems to me, however, that *hope* expresses the idea better, involving breadth (i.e., various areas of fulfillment) and depth (of experience), and all with a view to the appropriation of the truth.

14. Sasson offers the following interpretation of the events: "In 2:3b the narrator observes that Ruth 'happened to come to the part of the field belonging to Boaz.' In view of the story's stress on God's providential guiding of the lives of this family, it is surprising to find such a crucial item in the pattern of events which brought Ruth and Boaz together attributed to chance. Such a secular point of view is startling, to say the least. How can the same writer trace a chain of events whose beginning (1:6) and ending (4:13) are found in God's all-causality, and then describe one of the links in the middle of that chain as accidental? The answer, of course, lies in the subtlety of the writer's style. Surprising as it may seem at first glance, the author's real meaning in 2:3b is actually the opposite of what he says. The labeling of Ruth's meeting with Boaz as 'chance' is nothing more than the author's way of saying that no human intent was involved. For Ruth and Boaz it was an accident, but not for God. The tenor of the whole story makes it clear that the narrator sees God's

hand throughout. In fact, the very secularism of his expression here is his way of stressing that conviction. It is a kind of underplaying for effect. By calling this meeting an accident, the writer enables himself subtly to point out that even the 'accidental' is directed by God.

Ruth had come with a request that could not be fulfilled by a mere overseer. All that he could do is ask her to step aside and wait until the 'boss' arrived. In this way Ruth was assured of meeting Boaz, since the latter could hardly fail to notice her as she stood by" (pp. 44, 48).

15. Cox, p. 88; Taylor, p. 46.
16. R. de Vaux, *Early History of Israel*, pp. 717-27.
17. L. Kohlberg, *Collected Papers on Moral Development and Moral Education* (San Francisco: Harper & Row, 1973-   ), in process.
18. de Vaux, pp. 30-35.
19. Taylor, pp. 37-38.
20. *Wehinnēh-bōᶜaz bāʾ*, "And look, Boaz came," shows that the string of imperfects with the *waw* consecutive (v. 3) is interrupted by the word "Look." It is a graphic and vivid way of focusing the reader's attention on something new that is taking place.
21. Although some commentators find no reason to see in these greetings an expression of a pious attitude (cf. H. Gunkel, *Ruth, Reden and Aufsätze* [1913], pp. 65-92), and advance as their reason the Arabic *Allah maᶜ akum* ("Allah be with you") and the answer *Allah yaḥphaḍak* ("may Allah protect you"), such reasoning fails to account for Boaz's use of the most revered name for God among the Hebrews, *Yahweh*. If *Elohim* had been used, we would concur with the weight of scholarly opinion.

But what are we to make of the response of the reapers (who also used the name *Yahweh*) and Boaz's subsequent statement to them to have a "hands off" policy where Ruth is concerned? Surely their standard of morality should be in keeping with their religious profession. A possible answer to this dilemma may be found in their evident courtesy. Their employer Boaz had used a term implying great respect for God, and they may have used the same term out of respect for him.

22. See Morris, p. 271.
23. Sasson, p. 46.
24. There is no article with "Moabitess" and the overseer gives no name to the woman he is describing. By these gestures he implies that she is insignificant and of no social account.
25. *Wattōʾmer ʾalaqqotāh-nnāʾ weʾāsaptî bāᶜomārîm ʾaharēy haqqôṣerîm*, "And she asked, 'Please let me glean, and I will gather among the sheaves, after the reapers.'" Commentators have puzzled over Ruth's request. To glean in among the sheaves was not permitted, or was viewed as a special favor (see 2:15). Was this a problem of Ruth's dialect or did the overseer improperly understand Ruth's request? Is it also possible that Ruth may have

had a deficient understanding of what the law permitted? Or is it that Ruth requested to be allowed to gather up what had been left behind by the reapers, working in between the bound sheaves? Joüon, *Ruth* (p. 49), prefers to amend the text so that ʿomārîm, "sheaves," is changed to ʿamîrîm, "swath, row of fallen grain." Such attempts to explain interpretative problems inherent in the text are at best doubtful expedients.

26. *Mēʾ az habbōqer weʿad- ʿattāh zeh*, "since the morning even until now" or "from early morning until now," is a temporal phrase. The question posed by grammarians is whether this phrase goes with the second part of the sentence. If so (and the pointing of the MT indicates that it should), then the emphasis is to be placed upon the diligence with which Ruth stuck to her task.

27. See Cox, pp. 88-89.

28. What was the nature of this *habbayit*, "and she sat"? W. Reed, *College of the Bible Quarterly* 41 (1964), p. 8, believes it was a latrine. R. A. Knox, *The Old Testament, Newly Translated from the Vulgate* (New York: Sheed and Ward, 1948-50), 1:378, translated this as if Ruth had not returned to her home. It seems preferable to see this "shelter" as a temporary structure made of upright poles and roofed with branches or straw. Those in need of rest could sit in its shade.

29. Antoinette Wilson, "Wit's End Corner."

30. See Gary H. Strauss, "What Ever Happened in Eden?" *Psychology for Living* 17 (Dec. 1976), pp. 18-19 for a discussion of the elements of our security, how these were lost at the time of the Fall, and the manner in which they are restored to us when we believe in Christ.

Chapter 4

1. This illustration appeared later in Swindoll's timely book *Make Up Your Own Mind . . . About the Issues of Life* (Portland, Oreg.: Multnomah, 1981), pp. 66-67. See also Charles A. Goodrum's *Treasures of the Library of Congress* (New York: Harry N. Abrams, 1980), p. 280.

2. See the author's *God Has the Answer . . .* (Grand Rapids: Baker), pp. 11-21.

3. Boaz is not spoken of as an Ephrathite (cf. 1:2). He was not a part of the wealthy aristocracy.

4. Watson, p. 390.

5. This sentence, beginning with *halôʾ šāmaʿt bittî*, "do you not hear, my daughter," is interrogative in nature and expresses a *positive* wish. The *bittî*, "my daughter," is regarded by many commentators as evidence of the disparity between their ages. The word really means "young lady," and there is no reason to believe that Boaz was more than ten years older than Ruth.

6. The addition of the word *gam*, "also," which seems superfluous, preserves a quaint, archaic manner of speech, and gives tacit proof that, as Morris has observed, "It does not seem as though the main facts recorded have to do with the remote past" (p. 239).

7. The expressions "do not leave . . . you shall stay . . ." are emphatic. The former uses *lō* instead of the more common ʿal, and the latter employs an

unusual preposition, *dābaq ᶜim* after "you shall stay." See also 1:14, 2:21, 23. It seems to give evidence of Boaz's special way of speaking. Kennedy says, "Of the seven examples of this archaism, four are in Ruth (ii. 8, 21, iii. 4, 18), suggesting that the author of this book wished to give an archaic colour to this (*viz*, Boaz') style, *to suit the period of the story*" (p. 31, italics added). With this last statement we cannot agree.

8. This sentence lacks a verb and has been variously translated "Keep your eyes on the field," or with emphasis on "and you shall *go*," rendering the Hebrew, "Keeping your eyes on the field, go out after them. . . ." The latter translation ignores the *waw*, "and," and forces an unnatural construction upon the sentence.

9. The verb *yiqṣōrūn*, "they shall harvest," is masculine, whereas "after them" uses a feminine plural suffix. That would seem to imply that both men and women were involved in harvesting. It is possible that the men cut the crop and the women tied the stalks into bundles. Joüon, *Ruth* (p. 53) disagrees with this and believes that the feminine form is a textual error. He is hard pressed to maintain his theory, for the feminine form also occurs in 2:8, 9, 22-23, and 3:2.

10. "And you shall go . . ." is here equivalent to an imperative.

11. "Have I not ordered the young men not to touch you," *halōʾ ṣiwwîttî ʾet-hanneᶜ ārîm lebiltî nogᶜek,* has caused many commentators to debate the meaning of *nāgaᶜ,* "to molest." Sasson (p. 50) does not believe Ruth ran any risk of being sexually assaulted. See *TWOT*, 2:551; BDB, p. 619. Morris writes, "One can imagine that the enthusiasm of the gleaners would cause them to encroach on the legitimate property of the owners of the crops unless they were checked, and that accordingly the reapers might repulse, by force, if necessary, any who came too near before the owners were through. Ruth would know this and keep her distance. Boaz' instruction to Ruth enabled her to work close to the reapers in a position specially favourable for gleaning. But this very position exposed her to the possibility of rude jests and even mishandling from the workmen. He now tells her that he has guarded against this by giving instructions to the reapers that they were to leave her alone. His order would allow her to approach before other gleaners and thus ensure that she obtained a good reward for her labours, and this without being treated disrespectfully" (p. 275). Against these views is the use of *lebiltî* (see 1:13 and 3:10), which implies a strong prohibition against anything that might lead up to Ruth's being molested.

12. Harvesting was thirsty work. Joüon, *Ruth* (pp. 53f.) believes the content of those skins was wine. The verb "have drawn," however, as Campbell notes, "is used exclusively for drawing water" (p. 98)—probably from the well of Bethlehem from which David, years later, would wish to drink (2 Sam. 23:15-16).

13. *Hithpaᶜel*, "she prostrated herself."

14. *Lehakkîrēnî weʾ ānōkî nokriyāh*, "that you should notice me, and I a

stranger," employs the *Hiph͑ il* infinitive construct with the meaning of "to observe (with a view to recognition); *we͗ ānōkî,* "and I," according to Myers (p. 19ff.), is further evidence for the early date of Ruth, for otherwise the shorter *͗anî* would have been used; and finally, *nokriyāh,* with the preceding pronominal suffix, forms a circumstantial noun clause.

15. The word "fully" stands at the beginning of the sentence indicating, by means of the word order, the emphasis designed by the writer. *Huggēd huggad,* are *Hoph͑als* of *ngd* and, as Campbell reminds us, are a "mark of classical Hebrew prose" (p. 99).

16. Hebrew, "yesterday and the third day." See Morris, p. 276.

17. *Yešallēm YHWH po͑olēk,* "may *Yahweh* repay your work," is unusual for there is no preposition or mark of the accusative. The usage of *po͑olēk,* "deeds, work, actions," is often found in Hebrew poetry, and always in the early period of Israel's literary history.

18. The reference to Yahweh's "wings," *kenapāyw,* recalls Deuteronomy 32:37. "The metaphor," says Fuller, "is borrowed from a hen, which, with her clucking, summons together her straggling chickens, and then outstretcheth the fan of her wings to cover them" (pp. 139-40).

19. The use of the imperfect expresses a wish, "may I find."

20. Morison says, "To be one of [Boaz's] maidens was, in her estimation, to be a most desirable condition. She could not aspire to that. But as he had spoken so graciously to her heart, and soothed its sorrows, she trusted he would still befriend her" (p. 37). Boaz had done all this for her even though she was not one of his maids.

21. Morris, p. 277.

22. G. C. Morgan, *Living Messages of the Books of the Bible,* pp. 134-36.

23. Some translators (Luther, Coverdale, KJV) took the words "at mealtime" to be a part of what Boaz said to Ruth: "And Boaz said, 'At mealtime come here, and you shall eat.'" The punctuation of the MT seems to favor the translation we have adopted. Joüon, *Ruth* (pp. 57-58) observes that the dramatic effect of Ruth's words (v. 13) would be utterly lost if Boaz's immediate reply to her was that she concern herself with the mundane matter of food. This need not be so, for Boaz's invitation was further evidence of his concern.

24. W. M. Thompson in *The Land and the Book* (Grand Rapids: Baker, 1966) says: "A quantity of the best ears, not too ripe, are plucked with the stalks attached. These are tied into small parcels, a blazing fire is kindled with dry grass and thorn bushes, and the cornheads are held in it until the chaff is mostly burned off. The grain is thus sufficiently roasted to be eaten, and it is a favourite article all over the country" (p. 648).

The *ḥōmeṣ,* "vinegar," (sometimes a liquid and sometimes a thin paste) could be either fresh or fermented (cf. Num. 6:3). In Psalm 69:21 the term is used for the kind of drink a thirsty man would not want.

When Boaz invited Ruth to sit "beside" *(miṣṣad)* his workers (i.e., within the circle), he was demonstrating in a dramatic way that she was to be accepted as one of the group. When he himself served her, he was showing that to him she was a person worthy of such honor.

25. "And he reached to her," *wayyiṣboṭ-lāh*, occurs only here. The verb is thought to be derived from the Akkadian *ṣābātu*. It bears a similarity to *sebātîm* (2:16) and, according to some philologists, is an eastern Semiticism that found its way into early Hebrew usage.

   The three verbs, *wattōˀkal wattiśbaˁ wattōtar*, "and she ate, and was satisfied, and had some left over," are linked by three *waw* consecutives. They emphasize Boaz's generosity.

26. "Roasted grain," *qālî*, was a staple in the diet of the poorer people. See *TWOT*, 2:798-99.

27. "The Massoretes note that this is one of some 80 instances where pathach remains without the pausal lengthening 'at the end of a verse' " (Kennedy, p. 37).

28. The jussive here conveys the idea of "Let her glean (even between the sheaves)."

29. The *hiphˁil* imperfect, *taklîmûhā*, "shame, humiliate, disgrace," has caused commentators difficulty. Thompson in *The Land and the Book* (p. 648) states he had observed the kind of behavior that characterized the harvesting process, and that verbal abuse was the least of the offenses. Campbell says the use of this word "underscores Boaz' determination to protect Ruth from improper advances from the men" (p. 103). That Boaz gave instruction personally to *all* his men and did not content himself with an order to his overseer seems to imply something serious. Sasson (p. 56), and Joüon, *Ruth* (pp. 60-61) feel the import of the words is too strong and prefer to amend the text (changing the root from *klm* to *klˀ*).

30. *Biblical Researches*, 2:394.

Chapter 5

1. Mortimer Adler, *Six Great Ideas* (New York: Macmillan, 1981) p. 3.

2. James White, the London financier, had all that money could buy—material comforts, social position, and power—yet he had not found happiness. Ultimately he took his own life, and in a letter he left behind he said: "Gone are the nicer feelings and contentment. One day follows another with similar monotony. Life is just one drab day after another."

3. de Vaux, pp. 39-40; see also F. C. Fensham, "Widow, Orphan, and the Poor in Ancient Eastern Legal and Wisdom Literature," *JNES* 21 (1962), pp. 129-39; *TDOT*, 1:287-91.

4. The plural form appears in the text.

5. There is some confusion over whether these words should be translated "her mother-in-law saw" or "she showed her mother-in-law." Translators line up on both sides. Perhaps the only decisive evidence is the absence of *ˀet* before

"mother-in-law." This would seem to favor the translation we have adopted.

6. Literally, "from her satiety." This reveals both her hunger and Boaz's liberality.

7. Sasson (p. 58) treats *ʾēypōh liqqaṭṭ hayyôm weʾānāh ʿasit* as two different questions. He is influenced by Joüon, *Ruth* (p. 63), who considers the text to be faulty. Campbell points out that the text is to be regarded as synonymous parallelism "although the text as we have it connects the two questions with the conjunction 'and'" (p. 105). The *ʾēypōh* and *ʾānāh*, both asking the question "where," are much less frequent than *ʾayyēh* (though as BDB points out, *ʾayyēh* is never used with verbs).

8. The "power to bless" versus the "power to curse" is something that should not pass by unnoticed. The power to bless is essentially a characteristic of the Judeo-Christian religion. The power to curse is essentially pagan and was used when someone wanted to gain control over another. Its modern counterpart may be seen in threats, different forms of coercion, and malevolent manipulative devices. By way of contrast, invoking blessing upon another leaves the individual free to respond to God's leading without feeling obliged to continue to minister to our need.

9. Cox, p. 97.

10. Commentators have picked up on the supposed redundancy in "with whom she worked" and "with whom I worked." Some even point out that the LXX preserves the essence of Ruth's reply, but without the belabored repetition. But when it is borne in mind (1) that we are moving from indirect to direct discourse, (2) that when she identified the owner of the field it was necessary for Ruth to introduce him by referring back to Naomi's question, and (3) that in the recounting of the story the repetition adds emphasis and also delays the mention of Boaz's name (thus increasing the suspense), the effect gained fully justifies the process.

11. Campbell, p. 106.

12. "Living" (referring to Naomi and Ruth) is masculine plural. We would have expected a feminine plural. Inasmuch as the reference is to the *two* women, we have a similar situation to the one we drew attention to in Ruth 1 where we suggested that this may be an early form of "corporate" address.

13. See Morris, p. 280. With this, Cox (p. 98) is in essential agreement. Glueck, *Hesed in the Bible* (pp. 35ff.), believes that the clause modifies Boaz. Campbell says, "It is true that Boaz has done acts of *ḥesed* in chapter 2 and will yet do more, but the much more likely antecedent is Yahweh" (p. 106; cf. Gen 24:27).

14. Cox, pp. 98-99.

15. For the fullest explanation see Leggett, pp. 73-139 and 181-201; see also A. R. Johnson, "The Primary Meaning of *G'L*," *Studentenalmanak Vrije Universiteit* 1 (1953), pp. 71ff.

16. D. Daube, *Studies in Biblical Law* (New York: Ktav, 1947), pp. 44ff. Leggett cites the work of the Dutch theologian R. Sikkema, *De Lening in het Oude*

Testament (1957), pp. 95-111—a work that was not available to me.

17. I. Mendelsohn, "Slavery in the Ancient Near East," *BA* 9 (1946), pp. 74-88; H. L. Ellison, "The Hebrew Slave," *EQ* 45 (1973), pp. 30-35; Morris, pp. 282-83.

18. M. Buttenweiser, "Blood Revenge and Burial Rites in Ancient Israel," *JAOS* 38-39 (1918), pp. 306ff.; J. Porter, "Legal Aspects of Corporate Personality," *VT* 15 (1968), pp. 365ff.

19. G. A. Cooke, *The Book of Ruth*, pp. 3-4; J. Mittelman, *Der altisraelitische Levirat* (Leiden: Ginsberg, 1934), p. 18; L. Epstein, *Marriage Laws in the Bible and the Talmud*, pp. 85ff.

20. See Leggett, pp. 181-88.

21. Ruth still is referred to as a Moabitess. Many commentators point out that such repetition is unnecessary. See J. de Waard and E. A. Nida, *Translation of the Book of Ruth* (New York: United Bible Societies, 1973), p. 43. Others make a rather clumsy apology for it. Campbell remarks, "If it is redundant to have 'the Moabitess' expressed, it is equally redundant to repeat 'to her mother-in-law'" (p. 107). The solution to this persistent, purposeful repetition must be found in the author's intent and theme. Ruth has no claim to the *gōʾēl* rites of Israel. Naomi has no right to expect her daughter-in-law to support her. By God's grace alone, Boaz will act according to the spirit of the law and contract a *geʾullah* marriage with Ruth, who will engage in such a marriage for the sake of Naomi.

22. The reference to *hanneʿārîm*, "young men," has led some to conclude that Ruth's libidinal drives were leading her away from her commitment to Naomi, and that she was indeed thinking that marriage to one of them might be a means of escape from her present problems. Morris (p. 281), however, offers the suggestion that this term included *all* those engaged in the harvest, men as well as women. In verse 22 Naomi uses *naʿarôtāyw*, "young women," (see v. 8) and this strengthens the view that *hanneʿārîm* refers to both sexes.

23. The use of *yipgeʿû-bāk*, "attack, fall upon," has been subject to a variety of interpretations. In Joshua 2:16, 1 Sam. 22:17-18, and 1 Kings 2:25-46 the word appears in its normal usage of "to strike down, to attack violently." Although it is true that the context frequently determines the meaning, there is no indication here that Ruth's personal safety was *not* an issue. Morris (pp. 281-82) and Sasson (p. 62) do not believe that Ruth ran any risk. Campbell, however, says, "Naomi's instructions do appear to place more emphasis on Ruth's personal safety, although no other use of the word in the OT suggests sexual assault. Nevertheless, by this slight change of verb, from *ngʿ* to *pgʿ*, the storyteller may be nudging his audience along to think about the protection of the 'elect' woman" (p. 108).

24. The reconstruction of the calendar of the ancient Hebrews has been made possible by the discovery of the Gezer Calendar (c. 925 B.C.). According to Deuteronomy 16:9-12 it seems evident that the time from the beginning of

the barley harvest to the end of the wheat harvest was normally seven weeks, culminating in the Feast of Pentecost. W. F. Albright, in *Ancient Near Eastern Texts* (p. 320), and in an article in the *BASOR* 92 (Dec. 1943), pp. 25ff., and G. E. Wright, in *Biblical Archaeology* (Philadelphia: Westminster, 1962), pp. 183ff., have shown that the precise time of the beginning of the harvest would differ. The grain of the higher elevations would ripen sooner than the grain on the lower elevations. In addition, there would also be a slight difference in the ripening of grain from south to north. The general time of harvest, however, ran from late April to early June.

25. Cox, pp. 99-100.

Chapter 6

1. *Conceptions of Modern Psychiatry* (New York: W. W. Norton, 1940), pp. 42-43.
2. *Levirate and Goel Institutions in the Old Testament*, pp. 55, 58.
3. "Have I not been seeking . . . " and "is not Boaz our relative . . . " are illustrations of the Hebraic way of using the "abstract for the concrete" (i.e., of stating something in a positive way). See Wright, p. 40. The imperfect form of the first verb implies an active, continuous effort on Naomi's part.

   Campbell (p. 116) draws attention to this negative form of rhetorical question with the addition of "daughter," and links it with 2:8-9 and 3:10 to conclude that because they spoke the same way, Naomi and Boaz were the same age. Such a conclusion bears consideration. Campbell overlooks certain facts, namely (1) the use of the word "daughter" in situations where one who is a social superior is addressing a social subordinate, (2) the use of the perfect tense of the verb in 2:8-9, whereas in 3:1 we have the imperfect, and (3) the possibility that such an expression could easily have been a form of provincialism without having any bearing on one's age. These issues need to be considered before any decision is reached regarding Boaz's age.
4. The word here is *mānôaḥ*, a cognate of *menûḥâh* (1:9). It implies passively the "rest" a woman enters into when she is spared all the nagging insecurities of life; and actively, the security and benefits that accrue to a woman who enters marriage. The meaning is reinforced by Naomi's "that it may be well with you."
5. The use of *mōdaʿtānû*, "our kindred," has posed problems for interpreters. The word comes from the root *ydʿ*, "to know." It appears in the text as a feminine noun, and the suffix *-ānu* (instead of the expected *-ēnu*) is analymous. Its meaning is clear; Campbell (pp. 117f.) discusses the grammatical and syntactical problems.
6. The meaning of *gōren*, "threshing floor," has been the subject of considerable debate. The structure of the sentence, *himmēh-hûʾ zōreh ʾet-gōren haśśeʿōrîm hallāyelāh*, "he is the one who winnows the threshing floor of barley," has led many to question the accuracy of the text. Ruth 2:23 mentions the wheat harvest following the barley harvest. Why then had the

grain not been winnowed at the time of harvesting? Assuming the correctness
of the text, where had the grain been kept? Also, where was the threshing
floor?

In answer to the first question, it is possible that the harvested bundles of
barley were brought either into the city or kept in some form of shelter until
the time of winnowing. Such structures, if not in the city, would probably
have been near the threshing floor, and from what we can deduce from the
history of the times, must have been closely guarded. If the reapers harvested
the wheat immediately after the barley there is no reason to doubt the
accuracy of the text, which identifies the activity here as involving the
winnowing of barley. Joüon, *Ruth,* tries to escape the difficulty by regarding
the clause as metonomic, "the product of the threshing floor" (p. 67). His
reasoning is inconclusive.

Second, Campbell (pp. 117-19) discusses the location of the threshing
floor at length. He proposes changing the text from *śeʿōrîm,* "barley," to
šeʿarîm, "gates" (ignoring the difficulty of whether the barley was winnowed
ahead of the wheat), and on the basis of passages like 1 Kings 22:10, places
the activity of the evening close to the gate of Bethlehem. His evidence for
such a practice being done in or near the gates of other cities is impressive. In
the context of Ruth 3, however, Naomi's *weyāradty,* "go down," would seem
to imply a place other than in or near the gate of the city, because the gates of
cities were normally situated on high ground (cf. 4:1).

7. The importance of *hallāyelāh,* "tonight," or "this very night," adds a sense
of urgency to Naomi's words. Her plan, conceived some six weeks
previously (2:20) and carefully worked out, now needs immediate execution.

The use of *laylāh,* "night," is not the same as *ʿereb,* "evening" (2:17).
Joüon, *Ruth* (p. 67) develops a case for regarding the "night" as being any
part of the afternoon (cf. Josh. 2:2ff.). Morris, whose judgment is balanced
and discriminating, says, "It is possible that the wind in the daytime was very
strong or very gusty, which would make winnowing difficult. If these were
the conditions, then work at night might well be preferable. L. P. Stone says
that in the summer the wind blows from about four or five o'clock until a little
after sunset" (p. 285).

Although not wishing to appear to contradict so worthy a commentator, I
observed, on a recent visit to the Holy Land, modern Israeli farmers in the
higher elevations and south of the Horns of Hattin winnowing grain at
midday. See D. Baly, *Geography of the Bible* (New York: Harper & Row,
1974), pp. 46, 64.

8. Joüon, *Ruth* states that "Ruth was to bathe and anoint herself with aromatic
oil" (p. 68). He refers to the apocryphal book of Judith (10:3) for support.
Campbell (p. 120) refers to the Septuagint and the Lucianic manuscripts,
which specify that she was to rub herself with myrrh. Biblical evidence for
"anointing oneself" may be found in Esther 2:12; Psalm 45:9; Proverbs 7:17,
and particularly in Song of Solomon 1:3, 13; 4:14; 5:1, 5, 13.

9. Some take *śimlāh,* "garment," to imply that Ruth had only one piece of

clothing (cf. Joüon, *Ruth,* p. 69). Others believe that she "put off her 'widow's weeds'" (e.g., Watson, p. 401). However, if Ruth had characteristically worn clothes that would identify her as a widow, then Boaz would not have asked to whom she belonged in 2:5. Because Ruth later is found to possess a *miṭpaḥat,* "cloak, shawl, covering," she may have possessed another dress (used on this occasion) that the Hebrew text has not alluded to heretofore (cf. 4:3 where Naomi has land not previously brought to the attention of the reader).

10. *Weyaradty,* "go down," should present no problem to the interpreter. Bethlehem is situated on a ridge jutting out from the mountain chain. It would be natural for people leaving the city to "go down" into the valley, unless they were going to Jerusalem six miles away, when the expression would be to "go up." Some writers, however, in an endeavor to link what takes place in this chapter with the sexual orgies associated with fertility rites, claim that Ruth "went up" to the high place to participate in these pagan activities. Cf. H. G. May, "Ruth's Visit to the High Place in Bethlehem," *JRAS* 75 (1939), p. 70; W. E. Staples, "The Book of Ruth," *AJSL* 53 (1937), pp. 155-57.

11. The use of *tiwwādeᶜî,* "to be known," is regarded by some as evidence that Naomi's plan involved Ruth's having sexual relations with Boaz. Although the verb *yādaᶜ* is used of "carnal knowledge," it must be remembered the *niphᶜal* never conveys that idea, whereas the *qal* may (depending on the context). See G. Coats, "Widows Rights: A Crux in the Structure of Genesis 38," *CBQ* 34 (1972), pp. 464ff.; S. Sherman and J. Curtis, "Divine Human Conflicts in the Old Testament," *JNES* 28 (1969), pp. 234-37; cf. J. Gray, *Joshua, Judges, Ruth,* p. 417.

12. The precise meaning of *wegillît margelôtāw,* "and uncover his feet," has received extensive comment from Campbell (p. 121), Joüon, *Ruth* (p. 69), and Sasson (pp. 69-71). E. Robertson, "The Plot of the Book of Ruth," *BJRL* 32 (1950), pp. 225, 228, portrays Naomi as a scheming, pragmatic woman who "outwitted" Boaz who, following the night on the threshing floor, found himself in a compromised position and was compelled to marry Ruth.

13. F. C. Fensham, "Widow, Orphan and the Poor in Ancient Near Eastern Legal and Wisdom Literature," *JNES* 21 (1962), pp. 129-39.

14. M. Weinfeld, "Ruth," *Encyclopedia Judaica* (New York: Macmillan, 1971), p. 520.

15. Morris, p. 287.

16. The use of *wattaᶜaś kekōl* is taken by most scholars to mean "she did everything exactly" as her mother-in-law had commanded her.

17. Campbell (p. 121) states that Ruth did exactly what Naomi told her to do—up to a point. Then, where Naomi had said "he will tell you what to do," Ruth instead graciously and with befitting courtesy suggested what he was to do. In this we see her desire to look out for Naomi's interests.

18. Harvest time was a time of feasting and enjoyment (cf. Isa. 9:3).

19. Sasson (p. 73) says that in Hebrew we frequently encounter *lēb,* "heart," used with a form of the root *ṭôb* or *yṭb,* "to be good," to describe various

forms of emotional well-being (cf. Isa. 9:2; 1 Kings 8:66; Prov. 15:15; Eccles. 9:7; Robinson, 1:50; 2:35, 83, 306ff.

20. See Joüon, *Ruth,* pp. 70-71.

21. For comments on the usage of *ballāṭ,* "quietly, secretly," see Joüon, *Ruth,* p. 71; Myers, p. 28; and the Hebrew text of Judges 4:21; 1 Samuel 24:5.

22. Confusion exists over the meaning of *wegillît margelôtāw,* "uncover his feet." In 3:7 it specifies what Ruth uncovers. In 3:8 and 14 it specifies where Ruth sleeps. In some other passages of Scripture it refers to the sexual organs of either men or women (cf. Judg. 3:24; 1 Sam. 24:3; 2 Kings 18:27 [Isa. 36:12]; Isa. 7:20; Ezek. 16:25). From what follows it appears that Boaz's feet are intended from the context.

23. The Hebrew is most expressive: "in the half of the night . . . " Boaz awoke, probably because of the cold, and when groping for the portion of his cloak that covered his feet, discovered a woman there.

24. The usage of *wayyeḥerad,* "shuddered, trembled," may have been on account of sudden fear or as a result of the cold. See Joüon, *Ruth,* pp. 71-72. (See also footnote 26 below.)

25. The Hebrew contains the feminine singular *ʾat.* Apparently there was sufficient light from the moon for Boaz to be able to vaguely discern a woman's form without being able to recognize her.

26. Commenting on Boaz's "who are you?", Sasson (pp. 76-78) conjectures that his superstitious nature caused him to fear the presence of the female demon *Lilith.* It would appear that he reads too much from pagan sources into the text of Ruth.

27. The word used here is *ʾāmāh,* "handmaid," and differs slightly from *šiphāh,* "maid-servant" (2:13), though the exact distinction between the two words is very slight. See A. Jepsen, "Amah and Schiphciah," *VT* 8 (1958), pp. 293-97; Morris, p. 289.

28. The use of *kenāpekā,* "wing," may refer back to 2:12. Some commentators, however, believe that the word refers to Boaz's "skirt" or the border of his cloak. The symbolism is the same regardless of whether *kenāpekā* is "wing" or "cloak." See *Theologisches Handworterbuch zum Alten Testament,* ed. E. Jenni and C. Westermann (Stuttgart: Verlag W. Kohlammer, 1971), 1:835. The issue revolves around whether *kenāpekā* is singular or a plural written defectively. The MT is singular, and reference to Deuteronomy 22:30 (Heb., v. 31); 27:20; and Ezekiel 16:8 seems to verify the assumption that the singular is correct.

29. The expression *kî gōʾel ʾattāh,* "for you [are] a redeemer," is significant. The article is absent; Ruth was either being very modest in her form of address (not wishing to press her claim too hard) or she was aware that there was a *gōʾēl* nearer of kin to Elimelech than Boaz.

30. We observe again the frequency with which the pious people of the story invoke the blessing of the Lord upon others. That is truly remarkable and stands in stark contrast to pagan belief and practice. See C. J. Barber and J. D. Carter, *Always a Winner* (Ventura, Calif.: Gospel Light, 1977), pp. 59-71.

31. Morris says: "The kindness *at the beginning* (KJV, RV) will be that which Ruth showed to Naomi in not forsaking her and in gleaning to provide for her needs. Now to this she has added a further evidence of her regard for family relationships. She has not followed natural inclinations (in seeking a young man in marriage), but has shown a responsible attitude to the family in looking to her gōʾēl as her marriage partner" (p. 290). It could also refer to Ruth's initial decision when she turned her back on her parents and homeland and chose to follow her mother-in-law. See Sasson, p. 84; Joüon, *Ruth*, p. 74.

32. The article is used with *baḥûrîm*, "the [choice] young men"—those who are handsome and in the prime of life. It stands in contrast to *neʿarîm*, "youths," and *zeqenîm*, "old men." Morris offers the following pertinent comment: "Boaz sees her faithfulness in the fact that when she thought of marriage Ruth did not go after *young men* . . . whether poor or rich. She preferred to keep to family connections and thus showed her respect for the right. She did not simply let her own personal inclinations rule her . . . . There is an article with *young men*. It is not 'young men' in general that is meant but 'the young men', the definite group of young men in the village. We should not overlook the implied compliment to Ruth. Boaz clearly was certain that had she wished Ruth might have married a rich young man. There would be no point in praising her faithfulness to family obligations otherwise" (p. 290).

33. The question again arises, How old was Boaz at the time of these events? We have before suggested that he was in his mid-thirties, older than Ruth yet younger than Elimelech would have been had he still been alive. To avoid having Boaz married to two women at once, the *Talmud* (Baba Bathra, 91a) has his wife die most opportunely at a time coinciding with Ruth's arrival in Bethlehem. We mention this to show how myths have developed around the person of Boaz. The *Midrash* (Ruth Rabba, III:10) depicts Boaz as an octagenarian. Rabbinic literature also sees Boaz dying as soon as Ruth has conceived (*Talmud*, Yalq. Shimʿoni, 608). Morris (pp. 290-91) and Rowley, "The Marriage of Ruth," *HTR* 40 (1947), pp. 78ff., believe him to be much older than Ruth. However, few men lived beyond their mid-forties in those times (though affluence did tend to prolong life), and when Boaz referred to Ruth as "my daughter" it does not mean that he was old enough to be her father.

34. The importance of "the gate" in the city life is attested by passages of Scripture such as Deuteronomy 5:14; 12:12; 14:21, 27-29; 15:7; 16:11, 14, 18; 17:2, 5, 8; 18:6; 23:16 (Heb., v. 17); 24:14; 26:12. See Campbell (p. 124); Morris (p. 291); W. M. Thompson, *Southern Palestine and Jerusalem* (London: T. Nelson, 1880), pp. 29-30.

35. The Hebrew ʾēšet ḥayil, "a woman of valor," is the same expression used to describe Boaz in 2:1, ʾîš gibbôr ḥayil, " a mighty man of valor," (except for the addition of *gibbôr*, "mighty"). Our preference in translating 2:1 was to see Boaz as a man of valor rather than riches, because here where the same word is used of Ruth, we know that she is in extreme poverty. The emphasis in both instances is on the quality of the person rather than on their

possessions. See Campbell (p. 125), Joüon, *Ruth* (p. 74), Morris (p. 291), and Sasson (pp. 87-88) for differing viewpoints.

36. *Weᶜattāh kî ʾomnām kî ʾim gōʾēl ʾānōkî,* "and now [it is] true that I [am] a redeemer," presents difficulties to the translator on account of the numerous particles and adverbs and the absence of verbs. Certain scholars (Campbell, p. 125; Myers, p. 25; Joüon, *Ruth*, pp. 74-75) delete certain words or amend the text. W. Staples, "Notes on Ruth 2, 20 and 3, 12," *AJSL* 54 (1937-38), p. 62, takes the ʾm to be a negative and regards Boaz's statement as a disclaimer: "But now, as a matter of fact, I am really *not* [your] gōʾēl." This view is contradicted by the evidence in Ruth 4.

37. See Watson, pp. 398, 402.

38. For a discussion of *lînî hallaylāh,* "stay tonight," and why certain letters have been printed in larger type, see Campbell (p. 125) and Sasson (pp. 88-89).

39. Morris (p. 203) points out that Boaz does not use the word *marry* when speaking of the other kinsman's rights. Boaz addresses himself rather to the responsibilities of a *gōʾēl*. However, his "I" (in "I will redeem you") is emphatic.

40. Campbell (p. 126) points out that the terminology here differs from the vocabulary of Deuteronomy 25:5-10. He conjectures that this was because Boaz knew his contemplated action did not conform exactly to the Mosaic statute but only adhered to its general intent. Boaz, however, may also have been quoting Deuteronomy 25 from memory.

41. The phrase *ḥay YHWH,* "as *Yahweh* lives," appears to be a standard form of oath. See G. Gerleman, *Theologisches Handwörterbuch zum Alten Testament,* 1:554-55.

42. Cited in Morris, p. 287.

43. Watson, p. 398.

44. Taylor, p. 77.

45. Sasson, p. 81; E. Neufeld, *Ancient Hebrew Marriage Laws,* pp. 31ff.; cf. *Talmud,* Baba Bathra, 91a.

46. See P. R. Ackerman and M. M. Kappelman, *Signals* (New York: Dial Press, 1978); M. Strommen, ed., *Five Cries of Youth* (New York: Harper & Row, 1974); and C. J. Barber and G. H. Strauss, *The Effective Parent,* for discussions of how parents may become more sensitive to their children's silent pleas.

47. C. J. Barber and A. A. Barber, *Your Marriage Has Real Possibilities* (San Bernardino, Calif.: Here's Life, 1981), pp. 1-11.

48. N. O'Neill and G. O'Neill, *Open Marriage* (New York: M. Evans, 1973).

49. *Saturday Review* 53 (March 1970), p. 23.

Chapter 7

1. *Harper's Magazine* 56 (Jan. 1976), pp. 75-78.

2. Morison observes: "The anonymous relative does not conceal the idea that it

would be only on the ground of doing what would be *for his own interest* that he could entertain for consideration the proposal of Naomi. He likewise assumed that if Boaz should be willing to act the kinsman's part, it would be simply because it could be turned to account *for his own interest.* He did not know that there was in Boaz's heart a love that truly 'seeketh not her own,' but in honour prefers the things of another" (p. 62).

3. The word translated "lay at his feet," *margelôtāw,* has been written defectively. We would have expected the addition of a yôd between the last two consonants. The importance of Ruth's action is that she took the same position as in verse 8. She did not cuddle up beside Boaz.

4. The Hebrew *wattāqom* is feminine, "and she arose." Joüon, *Ruth* (p. 77), proposes to change the text to read *wayyāqom,* "and he arose," to fit the statement which follows: "And Boaz said . . . . " Rudolph (p. 46) suggests the addition of *bidbārō,* "at his request," believing that this word has been lost. After due consideration of these proposals, I see no real reason for not following the biblical text.

5. The phrase *yaqqîr ʾîš ʾet-rēʿēhu,* "a man could recognize his neighbor," refers to that period of time preceding dawn when it is still too dark for one to discern any recognizable features. All that may be seen are shapes or silhouettes against the skyline. Morris (p. 203) draws our attention to a reference in the *Mishnah* (Yebamoth 2:8, Danby's translation, p. 220) in which a man is prevented from performing a levirate marriage if it is suspected that he has had sexual relations with a slave or a Gentile woman.

6. The article "the" appears in the text before the word "woman." Previously Boaz had spoken of Ruth as a *neʿārāh,* "young woman," or in more affectionate, familial terms as a *bat,* "daughter." Neither of these would now be appropriate. He and Ruth had committed themselves to each other and he had pledged to marry her. The word *ʾiššāh,* "woman," may also bear the meaning of "wife." The addition of the article would have been most appropriate, for Boaz had a specific person in mind.

7. Boaz's request for Ruth's cloak, *hābî hammiṭpaḥat ʾašer-ʿālayik,* is peculiar. Joüon, *Grammaire* (#75k [pp. 150-51]), and Myers (p. 18) offer suggestions regarding its etymology. It would seem to be an imperitival form of the root *yhb,* "to give" (cf. Ps. 55:22 [Heb. v. 23]). Campbell (p. 127) discusses the usage of the word based on its occurrence in other passages. Joüon, *Ruth* (p. 78) omits this phrase from his discussion and passes on to a consideration of the vocalization of *ʾehezî-bāh,* "and hold on to it." Boaz had Ruth assist him as he measured out six *seāh* of barley into her mantle.

8. A problem arises regarding how much barley Boaz gave Ruth. The Hebrew text, *wayyāmod šēš-śeʿōrîm,* "and he measured six [measures] of barley," leaves out the quantity. D. J. Wiseman, in "Weights and Measures," *IBD,* 3:1637-39, describes the Hebrew "dry measures of capacity": homer or *kor,* (220 liters); *ephah* (22 liters); *seah* (7.3 liters); and *omer* (2.4 liters). Although women in the Near East are used to carrying large loads, Boaz's

gift could not have been either six homers or ephahs. We are therefore left with either the *seāh* or the *ʿōmer*. Six *ʿōmer* of barley would have been less than Ruth had gleaned after spending all day in the field (cf. 2:17). That would have been a small gift to send to Naomi, particularly when the emphasis of the passage is on the sacrificial generosity of Boaz. Furthermore, *ʿōmer* is masculine whereas the adjective "six" is feminine. *Seāh,* however, is feminine and would better suit the syntax. When it is noted that Boaz had to lift the load onto Ruth, it is evident that something heavier than an *ʿōmer* is meant. Brockelmann, *Hebräische Syntax* (p. 77), lists passages in which an unspecified commodity (e.g., grain, oil, etc.) is used with only a numeral specifying amount. His classification of materials is helpful to the busy researcher even if some of his conclusions are misleading. For a fuller discussion see Campbell (p. 128), who proposes amending the text from *šeʿarîm* to *šeʿorîm,* an unknown and elsewhere unattested measure; Sasson (pp. 96-97), and de Vaux (pp. 200-203).

9. The purpose of Boaz's gift to Naomi has been variously explained: Paul Humbert, "Art et leçon de l'histoire de Ruth," *Révue de théologie et philosophie,* N.S. 26 (1938), pp. 257-86, proposes that this would give Ruth an excuse for her visit to the threshing floor. (He overlooks the fact that anyone seeing Ruth with such an accumulation of barley would think that she had come by it illegally.) Gunkel, *Ruth* (pp. 78f.) suggests that the barley was a symbolic gift assuring Naomi of Boaz's honorable intentions where Ruth was concerned; Rudolph (p. 57) believes that the gift to Naomi was repayment for her thoughtfulness of him in choosing him as her (and Ruth's) redeemer; Staples, "The Book of Ruth," *AJSL* 53 (1937), p. 57, advances the untenable theory that the six measures of barley were a gift to the grain god; May, in "Ruth's Visit to the High Place at Bethlehem," *JRAS* (1939), p. 78, regards Boaz's present to *Ruth* as payment for sexual favors. (He treats this in the same light as Judah's gift to Tamar, Gen. 38; cf. Hos. 9:1.) Rowley, "The Marriage of Ruth," *HTR* XL (1947), pp. 87-88, rebuts those false hypotheses.

   The *Midrash* (Ruth Rabbah, VII, 2) advances the equally improbable theory that six *seāhs* of barley was the minimum *mōhar,* or dowry, given to the parents of the bride. This is most unlikely for in passages like Leviticus 27:4-7, the minimum worth of a woman was set at thirty shekels of silver, and six measures of barley would have brought much less at the market. It seems preferable to see in this gift to Naomi a pledge on the part of Boaz to care for her and perform the responsibilities of a *gōʾēl.*

10. Most commentators and translators amend the text to "she," changing *wayyābō hāʿir,* "and he went to the city," to *wattābōʾ hāʿir,* "and she went to the city" (see Joüon, *Ruth,* p. 78; Morris, p. 295), claiming that "he" must be a scribal error. But we do not see why the MT should not be followed. Boaz went to the city, possibly to his house to obtain the necessary money, and Ruth returned to Naomi. Joüon's conjecture (p. 78) that Boaz was unlikely to have left the threshing floor overlooks the fact that there were other men there

who would have defended his harvest in the (unlikely) event of a raid (taking place so soon before dawn). The only problem to this view concerns the translation of 4:1. Does the verb look at the action as taking place (i.e., Boaz going up) or as Boaz already having gone to the city?

The circumstantial clause beginning with a *waw* conversive "then" followed by a perfect verb simply looks at the action that took place without indicating whether it was before, after, or contemporaneous with the events that have just been described; see KD, 4:487. For comments on the verb *ʿālāh*, "went up," see Joüon, *Ruth* (pp. 79-80), Campbell (pp. 140-41), and Sasson (p. 104). The writer of Ruth purposely avoided using the imperfect (which would have been expected).

It should be noted that in 4:1 Boaz "went up to the gate" (*not* to the city, as would be expected if he were leaving the threshing floor; cf. 3:15*b*). The impression left is that he went up to the gate from his house, for city gates were invariably situated at higher elevations when cities were built on hillsides, and only at lower levels if more than one gate led into the city. The gate of the city where the court convened, to which Boaz went, would obviously have been the chief entrance into the city situated on its most imposing elevation.

11. Naomi's greeting, *mî-ʾat bittî,* which literally means, "Who are you, my daughter," has been the subject of endless discussion. Morris (p. 295) believes that Naomi did not recognize Ruth when she knocked on the door of their cottage, but saw only the figure of a woman. This would be plausible but for the addition of the words "my daughter" (cf. Boaz's question in 3:9 where *bittî* is omitted). Joüon, *Ruth* (p. 78) and Rudolph (p. 57) take the *mî* as an "accusative of condition." Gerlemann (p. 34) takes *mî* to be an interrogative particle with the meaning of "Is it you?" For a more extensive discussion see Sasson, pp. 100-101. We have chosen the tentative translation, "How did things go, my daughter," but realize the subjectivity of this choice.

12. See Campbell (p. 129) and Sasson (pp. 101-2) for the various views regarding the significance of this gift to Naomi.

13. Naomi's *ʾēyk yippōl dābar* . . . and *kî-ʾim killah haddābār,* "how [the] matter falls" (i.e., turns out) . . . and "until he has completed the matter" (where *kî-ʾim* is used instead of *ʿad ʾašer*), seems to denote a condition that must be fulfilled before the preceding statement can be brought to completion. Morris (p. 296n) notes that the first *dābār* ("matter") lacks the article, whereas the second ("the thing") has it.

14. See S. L. Greenslade, *The Cambridge History of the Bible* (Cambridge: Cambridge U., 1963), 3:166, and G. MacGregor, *A Literary History of the Bible* (Nashville: Abingdon, 1968), p. 211.

15. The emphasis in the text is on the quantity of barley. Ruth apparently intended to stress Boaz's generosity as she recounted to Naomi the events of the night.

16. For a treatment of the function of city gates and their importance in the life of

the people, see W. M. Thompson, *The Land and the Book* (Hartford, Conn.: S. S. Scranton, 1910), 1:27-32; Morris, p. 297.

17. The term *wehinnēh haggōʾēl ʿōbēr*, "and, behold, the kinsman passing by," draws attention to the immediacy of what happened. Campbell (p. 141) translates *wehinnēh*, "and just then."

18. The imperatives contain the cohortative *ā*. It is the writer's way of adding emphasis. He reveals through this kind of literary device how deftly Boaz took command of the situation. Campbell adds, "Boaz acts with authority and at a determined pace" (p. 141).

I have omitted *pelōnî ʾalmōnî* from the translation because these Hebrew words virtually defy explanation. Some translate them "Such-and-such," or "So-and-so." Older writers felt that they were the equivalent of "John Doe," or some expression given in place of a personal name. The effect was to indicate someone who, for whatever reason, should not or could not be named. For an explanation of the different ideas behind this expression, see Sasson, pp. 105-7.

19. Evidently there were "elders" present as well as others "sitting [in the gate]," and Boaz includes the *yōšebîm*, "onlookers," out of courtesy. The emphasis comes from the repetition of *neged*, "before." See de Vaux, pp. 152-57.

20. Considerable discussion surrounds *mākerāh noʿomî*, "Naomi has sold." The issue concerns the interpretation of the verb as well as the question of Naomi's right to sell land.

Mākerāh is a perfect, feminine, third person singular verb. Wright (p. 55); KD (p. 488); and D. R. G. Beattie, "The Book of Ruth as Evidence for Israelite Legal Practice," *VT* 24 (1974), p. 19, translate this as describing action that has already taken place. S. R. Driver, *Treatise on the Use of the Tenses in Hebrew* (Oxford: Clarendon, 1881), says: "The perfect is employed to indicate actions, the accomplishment of which lies indeed in the future, but is regarded as dependent upon such an unalterable determination of the will that it may be spoken of as having actually taken place: thus a resolution, promise, or decree, especially a Divine one, is very frequently announced in the perfect tense. A striking instance is afforded by Ruth (iv. 3) when Boaz, speaking of Naomi's determination to sell her land, says [Mākrāh Nāʿōmî] literally, 'has sold' (has resolved to sell. The English idiom would be 'is selling')" (pp. 13-14). With this judgment A. B. Davidson, *Hebrew Syntax* (Edinburgh: T. & T. Clark, 1901), p. 41, is in essential agreement. The subsequent context (4:5, 9) indicates that the property had not been sold.

The issue surrounding Naomi's possession of land is not so easily resolved for, according to Numbers 27:8-11, the right to hold property passed through the male line. See J. Morgenstern, "The Book of the Covenant, Part II: *Hebrew Union College Annual* 7 (1930), p. 174; J. Weingreen, "The Case of the Daughters of Zelophehad," *VT* 16 (1966), p. 522; Z. Falk, *Hebrew Law in Bible Times* (Jerusalem: Wahrmann Books, 1964), p. 159; the extensive discussion by M. Burrows in "The Marriage of Boaz and Ruth," *JBL* 59 (1940), p. 448; K. H. Henrey, "Land Tenure in the Old Testament," *PEQ* 41

(1954), p. 9; and Leggett (pp. 211-22), alerts the reader to the complexity of the problem. Sasson (pp. 108-14) provides an evaluation of the various theories.

In answer to Rowley's question as to where Naomi suddenly acquired land after coming back to Judah penniless (see *HTR*, 40, p. 78), I offer the following explanation (also reached independently by Sasson), namely, that Elimelech and his family left Bethlehem at a time of severe famine. The fields were dry and perhaps had not been ploughed in more than a year. Elimelech did not plan to stay in Moab very long and probably left his plot of land in the care of a relative or friend. This individual undoubtedly was given the right to cultivate the land and harvest the crop as soon as conditions became favorable.

Elimelech's stay in Moab was longer than expected. In fact, more than ten years passed before Naomi returned. It was the harvest season and Naomi could not lay claim to the land and sell it while it was being harvested. Now that the threshing was over, Naomi proceeded with her plans to sell the portion of the field that once had been owned by Elimelech.

In the face of all the controversy over whether a widow could *legally* or *physically* own and sell land, the book of Ruth seems to indicate that whereas the Mosaic law laid down the basic principles by which God's people were to be governed, the latitude allowed the people was quite considerable (cf. 2 Kings 8:1-3, 6). The important point of the law was that the land remain in the family (or, if this failed, the tribe) and not pass into the hands of outsiders should a widow remarry.

21. This expression furnishes us with a fine example of the picturesque meaning of *lēʾmōr*, "I will open" or, as here, "uncover." The imagery is graphic and suggests the idea of slightly moving the hair so as to divulge to the listener something of great importance.

22. There is a change of person here as if Boaz, to keep the attention of those witnessing the proceedings, turned to them and said, "but if *he* will not redeem it." See Morison, p. 61; Morris, p. 303; and Sasson, p. 118.

23. The "I" is emphatic. It is as if Boaz knows that this unnamed relative is envious of Boaz's standing in the community and does not want anything to enhance Boaz's position. In emphasizing his willingness to redeem the land Boaz says in effect, "And I am right behind you," in order of kin. It seems as if the unnamed kinsman was glad to have the opportunity to add to his possession the property that belonged to Elimelech. However, as soon as Boaz introduced Ruth as a separate appurtenance of Elimelech's estate, a change came over the kinsman's feelings. He quickly remembered Boaz's statement "I am next in line after you" and availed himself of the means of escaping a difficult situation.

24. Verse 5 is permeated with perplexing interpretative problems. *Beyôm-qenôtekā haśśādeh*, "In the day of your acquiring [i.e., buying] the field," stresses the imminence of the act that the unnamed kinsman has agreed to

perform. *Beyôm* can also mean "at the time of" or "when" (see Joüon, *Grammaire,* #129 [p. 392]. See also de Vaux [pp. 180-81] for his discussion of time in the ancient Near East).

There is no problem translating *qānāh,* "to buy, purchase"; the difficulty comes in linking it with *ûmēᵉēt,* "then from" (Ruth). To purchase land simultaneously from two people is easy to imagine. The difficulty comes later on when the same word is used in connection with Ruth: *qānîtā lehāqîm šēm-hammēt ʿal-naḥalātô,* "you have 'bought' [her] to raise up the name of the dead on his inheritance." Does this verse imply that women were "bought" as brides? See Neufeld, *Ancient Hebrew Marriage Laws* (pp. 240ff.) D. H. Weiss, "The Use of *QNH* in Connection with Marriage," *HTR* 57 (1964), pp. 244-48, maintains that the verb *qnh* is only used in the Mishnah of marriage when other transactions are first involved (p. 246). See also M. Burrows "Levirate Marriage in Israel," *JBL* 59 (1940), pp. 23-33. With these considerations in mind, and for the sake of consistency, I chose to translate *qānāh* as "acquire."

A further complication concerns the *mem* in *mēᵉēt,* "to buy, purchase, acquire." Campbell (p. 146) regards it as enclitic; Sasson (pp. 120ff.) rejects this, amends *qānîtā,* "you purchase, acquire," to *qānîtî,* "I purchase, acquire," and thereby believes he has solved the problem. For a further discussion of the issues see T. and D. Thompson, "Some Legal Problems in the Book of Ruth," *VT* 18 (1968), pp. 79-99; and L. M. Epstein, *Marriage Laws in the Bible and the Talmud* (1942), pp. 81, 85-86, 114, 122.

25. de Vaux, pp. 21-22, 38.

26. The near kinsman's response, *lōʾ ʾûkal lgʾwl-lî,* "I am not able to redeem for myself," is most interesting. He does not say that he *will* not redeem the land, but that he cannot. The reason he gives is "lest I ruin my own inheritance." Note the "I . . . my . . . own." Joüon, *Ruth* (p. 84), believes that he is exaggerating the condition in which he will find himself. Beattie (p. 262) believes that the *gōᵉēl's* words imply nothing more than "I cannot afford it." Cassel, *Ruth,* however, believes the man to be superstitious: "It must be her Moabitish nationality that forms the ground, such as it is, of the kinsman's refusal. Elimelech's misfortunes had been popularly ascribed to his emigration to Moab; the death of Chilion and Mahlon to their marriage with Moabitish women. This it was that had endangered their inheritance. The *goël* fears a similar fate. He thinks that he ought not to take into his house a woman, marriage with whom was already been visited with the extinguishment of a family in Israel" (pp. 47-48). Most English commentators (who may have relied heavily on Lange's *Commentary* for their information) adhere to this view. See Cox, *Ruth,* pp. 138-40. In view of this kinsman's self-centeredness, it seems preferable to conclude that he did not want the responsibility of another wife and an addition to his family, with the sure knowledge that the field he was buying would in time pass out of his possession.

27. KD deals with the question of how Naomi came to possess Elimelech's

property. They say, "So far as the fact itself was concerned, the field, which Naomi had sold from want, was the hereditary property of her deceased husband, and ought therefore to descend to her sons according to the standing rule of right; and in this respect, therefore, it was Ruth's property quite as much as Naomi's. From the negotiation between Boaz and the nearer redeemer, it is very evident that Naomi had sold the field which was the hereditary property of her husband, and was lawfully entitled to sell it. But as landed property did not descend to wives according to the Israelitish law, but only to children, and when there were no children, to the nearest relatives of the husband (Num. xxvii. 8-11), when Elimelech died his field properly descended to his sons; and when they died without children, it ought to have passed to his nearest relations. Hence the question arises, what right had Naomi to sell her husband's field as her own property? The Rabbins suppose that the field had been presented to Naomi and Ruth by their husbands (*vid. Selden,* de success, in bona def. c. 15). But Elimelech could not lawfully give his hereditary property to his wife, as he left sons behind him when he died, and they were the lawful heirs; and Mahlon also had no more right than his father to make such a gift. There is still less foundation for the opinion that Naomi was an heiress, since even if this were the case, it would be altogether inapplicable to the present affair, where the property in question was not a field which Naomi had inherited from her father, but the field of Elimelech and his sons. The true explanation is no doubt the following: The law relating to the inheritance of the landed property of Israelites who died childless did not determine the time when such a possession should pass to the relatives of the deceased, whether immediately after the death of the owner, or not till after the death of the widow who was left behind (*vid.* Num. xxvii. 9 sqq.). No doubt the latter was the rule established by custom, so that the widow remained in possession of the property as long as she lived; and for that length of time she had the right to sell the property in case of need, since the sale of a field was not an actual sale of the field itself, but simply of the yearly produce until the year of jubilee. Consequently the field of the deceased Elimelech would, strictly speaking, have belonged to his sons, and after their death to Mahlon's widow, since Chilion's widow had remained behind in her own country Moab. But as Elimelech had not only emigrated with his wife and children and died abroad, but his sons had also been with him in the foreign land, and had married and died there, the landed property of their father had not descended to them, but had remained the property of Naomi, Elimelech's widow, in which Ruth, as the widow of the deceased Mahlon, also had a share. Now, in case a widow sold the field of her deceased husband for the time that it was in her possession, on account of poverty, and a relation of her husband redeemed it, it was evidently his duty not only to care for the maintenance of the impoverished widow, but if she were still young, to marry her, and to let the first son born of such a marriage enter into the family of the deceased husband of his wife, so as to inherit the redeemed property, and perpetuate the name and possession of the deceased in Israel. Upon this right, which was founded upon traditional custom, Boaz based this condition, which he set before the nearer redeemer, that if he redeemed the field of Naomi he must also take Ruth, with the obligation to marry her, and through this marriage to set up the name of the deceased upon his inheritance" (pp. 488-90).

28. *Aḥînû*, although translated "brother" (v. 3), has the extended meaning of "relative" or "kinsman" (i.e., someone from the same extended family), and may even be used of people who were not related (2 Sam. 1:26) or who had entered into a special covenant (Amos 1:9).

29. KD, 4:490.

30. Cox, p. 141.

31. Watson, p. 413.

Chapter 8

1. *Flamingo Road* (New York: Grosset and Dunlap, 1942).

2. See C. J. Barber, "Restoring God's Image in Man," *Theological Students Fellowship Bulletin* 71 (1975), pp. 17-20.

3. William Gesenius, *Hebrew and Chaldee Lexicon, Tregelles Translation* (Grand Rapids: Eerdmans, 1949), p. 293.

4. See C. C. Ryrie, *The Grace of God* (Chicago: Moody, 1963); cf. also R. M. Hals, *Grace and Faith in the Old Testament* (Philadelphia: Fortress, 1980).

5. G. A. Cooke, *Ruth*, is most certainly in error when he states, "When *property was transferred*, as in the present case, to take off the sandal and hand it to the person in whose favour the transfer is made, gave a symbolic attestation to the act and invested it with legal validity" (pp. 16-17, italics original). The unnamed kinsman transferred his rights to Boaz, not the property. The property had not yet been purchased from Naomi.

6. The word *leqayyēm*, "to confirm," is thought to be an Aramaism (see Joüon, *Ruth*, p. 85). Myers (p. 19), however, points out that several middle weak forms are found in the *Piel* as early documents. See also Campbell (p. 148) and Sasson (p. 142).

7. The statements *šālap ʾîš naʿalô*, "a man would draw off his sandal" (v. 7), and *wayyišlōp naʿalô*, "and he drew off his sandal" (v. 8), are worthy of close consideration. Morris (p. 308) reminds us that some Greek versions (LXX and Aquila) add, "and gave it [the sandal] to him [Boaz]." However, the question is not resolved that easily. Some commentators believe it was Boaz who gave away his shoe; others hold to the theory that they exchanged footwear. Joüon, *Ruth* (p. 88) believes that something has fallen out of the text through transmission. Campbell (p. 149) and Rudolph (p. 60) offer suggestions for this scribal omission. It seems preferable to conclude on the basis of Deuteronomy 25:9 that Boaz was the recipient of his relative's shoe.

8. The word *teʿûdāh*, "attestation, witness," is rare, occurring only here and in Isaiah 8:16, 20. Its meaning in Ruth differs from its usage in Isaiah. For an

explanation of its etymology, see Campbell (p. 149) and Sasson (p. 146). Morris says, "The custom is described simply. To confirm whatever was agreed upon, one man drew off (the tense is perfect; one might have expected a frequentative imperfect, but the perfect accords with the fact that the action was performed once only in each case) his sandal and gave it to the other. It is a curious custom, but at least its unusualness would mean that it attracted attention, and this probably was its object" (p. 306).

9. See de Vaux, pp. 22, 169; and C. M. Carmichael, "A Ceremonial Crux: Removing a Man's Sandal as a Female Gesture of Contempt," *JBL* 96 (1977), pp. 321-26.

10. Watson asks, "In buying the field and adding it to his estate will the man take Ruth to wife, to raise up the name of the dead upon his inheritance? He is not prepared to do that, for the children of Ruth would be entitled to the portion of ground, and he is unwilling to impoverish his own family" (p. 415).

11. See p. 85. Most commentators overlook the fact that this unnamed kinsman was ignorant of Naomi's plight. He was unaware that her poverty was compelling her to sell the land she and Elimelech had at one time farmed together.

12. Morison, p. 62; also Morris, p. 306.

13. The Hebrew has only the word ʿēdîm, "witnesses." See G. M. Tucker, "Witnesses and 'Dates' in Israelite Contracts," *CBQ* 28 (1966), pp. 42-45.

14. On Boaz's remarks (v. 9) see T. and D. Thompson, "Some Legal Problems in the Book of Ruth," *VT* 18 (1968), pp. 79-99; Sasson, p. 144.

15. Boaz's emphasis is clear. ʾEt-rût hammôʾabiyyāh ʾēšet maḥlôn qānîtî lî leʾiššāh, "and Ruth the Moabitess, the wife of Mahlon, I have acquired for myself for my wife." Ruth stands first in the sentence for emphasis. And here for the last time she is mentioned as "the Moabitess." From now on the people of Bethlehem will refer to her as "Ruth the wife of Boaz."

16. See Campbell, pp. 151-52.

17. G. A. F. Knight, *Ruth and Jonah* (1966), p. 37.

18. See S. P. Parker, "The Marriage Blessing in Israelite and Ugaritic Literature," *JBL* 95 (1976), pp. 23-30.

19. The perfect tense is used for something that has not yet taken place. This is not uncommon in Hebrew. See Campbell, pp. 152-53.

20. Such a comment was most gracious, and to be bestowed upon a foreigner was most unusual. Note Genesis 29:35 and the comments of Sasson (p. 154).

21. See Campbell, p. 152.

22. See Sasson, pp. 154, 156.

23. See Morris, p. 311.

24. The reference to Ruth as naʿarāh, "young woman," is translated by Campbell (p. 154) as "young girl" in an endeavor to prove the difference in age between Ruth and Boaz. Whatever difference in age that may be implied by the word, that difference is most properly applied to the span of years separating the elders of the city and Ruth. Being the grayhaired, venerable men of Bethlehem, they doubtless saw Ruth as being very young.

25. See J. Hastings, *Encyclopedia of Religion and Ethics* (Edinburgh: T. & T. Clark, 1908), 4:367ff.
26. *TWOT,* 1:132.
27. See J. D. Pentecost's *Things to Come* (Grand Rapids: Zondervan, 1964), pp. 433-45 for an explanation of the theocracy and the ability of God's theocratic representatives to pronounce blessing on someone.
28. KD, 4:491.
29. Morris, p. 312.
30. Ibid.
31. This conclusion is also reached by P. Humbert, "Art et leçon de l'historie de Ruth," *Opuscules d' un Hebraïsant* (1958), who affirms that after considering all the events that take place in this book, "the chief actor is God" (p. 108).
32. Taylor, p. 91.

Chapter 9

1. The term was coined by L. Penning and is the title of his 1954 (English translation) biography of the Genevan Reformer.
2. See P. Schaff, *History of the Christian Church* (Grand Rapids: Eerdmans, 1960), 8:360-61. (The quotation I have used comes from a sermon by Charles H. Spurgeon.)
3. For an explanation of the covenant see J. D. Pentecost's *Things to Come,* pp. 65-128.
4. Ibid, pp. 456-63.
5. The interim form of the Kingdom is explained in the parables of Matthew 13. See Pentecost, pp. 138-55, and R. C. Stedman, *Behind History* (Waco, Tex.: Word, 1976), p. 166.
6. The theocracy—one of the most important and least understood aspects of God's revelation—has been treated by Pentecost, pp. 433-511.
7. C. P. B. Weiss, *Biblical Theology of the New Testament,* trans. D. Eaton (Edinburgh: T. & T. Clark, 1885), 1:144.
8. Evidence of God's grace is found in the way Ruth is described by the writer. *Wattehî-lô leʾiššah,* "and she [Ruth] became to him [Boaz] a wife" (4:13). The emphasis of the sentence is on the word "wife." As we trace the writer's terms used to describe Ruth we find that she passes from a *nokriyyāh,* "stranger" (2:10), to a *šiphāh,* "handmaid" (2:13), and finally to an *iššah,* "wife" (4:13). Sasson (p. 161) points out that she was worthy enough to marry a *gibbôr ḥayil* ("a mighty [man] of valor") of Boaz's stature, becoming his *wife* and not merely his concubine or a handmaiden.
9. The question arises, Who was this *gōʾēl,* "kinsman," Boaz or Obed? Sasson (p. 163) conjectures that after the birth of his son, Boaz was no longer regarded as the *gōʾēl* and that technically the responsibility for Naomi's support fell on Obed. See Morris, p. 313. However, it is difficult to think of an infant assuming the support of his grandmother, unless the reference here is to position as opposed to performance (i.e., the assuming of a de jure

responsibility with Boaz still performing the role of a de facto *gōʾēl*). See J. Bewer, "The Goel in Ruth 4:14, 15," *AJSL* 20 (1903-4), pp. 202-6; Leggett, pp. 255-65; Rudolph, p. 69.

10. *Weyiqqarēʾ šemô beyiśrāʾēl*, "and may his name be called in Israel," conveys the idea of the development of a good reputation. For further comments, see Campbell, p. 163. Joüon, *Ruth* (p. 93), suggests that it is Naomi's husband, Elimelech, that is being referred to. In view of the emphasis of this verse as well as the one following, it would seem as if Obed is the one referred to.

11. The Hebrew *"wehāyāk lāk lemēšîb nepeš,* "a restorer of life" (there is no "your" in the Masoretic text as in the KJV), probably refers to the comfort and consolation Obed will bring to Naomi. God in His grace will have recompensed her for the loss of her sons. Campbell states, "Most noteworthy here is that the storyteller picks up the dominant key of the first chapter, *šwb,* 'to return,' especially as it is used in 1:21: 'empty Yahweh has brought me back' (or, 'caused me to return'). The signal is given: Naomi's complaint, dormant since 1:20-21, is here resolved" (p. 164).

12. *Kî kallātēk ʾašer-ʾahēbatek yelādattû,* "for your daughter-in-law, who loves you, has borne him," is of interest philologically as well as theologically. After *kî* one expects the verb before the subject. Here the subject comes first, probably for the sake of added emphasis. Sasson (p. 167) offers an explanation that he hopes will resolve the tension between the supposed "two-fold etiological narrative" that has been combined into the story of the "Birth of Obed." His comments are unconvincing and based upon the presumption of two sources for the information. Joüon, *Ruth* (p. 94), escapes the problems of the text by changing *ahēbatek* to *ʾahēbātek*. Theologically, we see God's grace at work, for Ruth (a foreigner) has succeeded in providing Naomi with an heir to Elimelech's (and Mahlon's) estate. That was something Naomi deemed to be impossible (cf. 1:11-12).

13. The debate over *wattešitēhu beḥēyqah,* "and laid him in her bosom," seems incapable of solution. Central in the discussion is whether this was merely an act of affection (cf. 1 Kings 3:20) or a legal sign of adoption. The Hebrew words for breast or bosom are varied and colorful. They are used of men as well as women (cf. 2 Sam. 12:3); and, as Campbell (p. 165) reminds us, are employed of "God's shepherding his lambs" (Isa. 40:11).

Yet the NASB translates *ḥeyq,* "lap." (For an explanation of Israel's adoption procedures see Z. Falk, *Hebrew Law in Bible Times,* pp. 163f.; E. Neufeld, *Ancient Hebrew Marriage Laws,* p. 126, n. 1; de Vaux, p. 51; Rudolph, pp. 70-71.) A possible solution for this rendering of the Hebrew may be found in the article by H. A. Hoffner, Jr., "Birth and Name-Giving in Hittite Texts," *JNES* 27 (1968), pp. 198-203. He shows that the placing of a child on the knee was equivalent to conferring upon him official recognition and legitimization. Joüon, *Ruth* (p. 94), however, sees no reason for Naomi to either adopt (or legitimize) a child who is considered to be Mahlon's and will inherit his estate. Gerleman (p. 37) advances the theory that Naomi's act is a "special type of adoption." However, he fails to provide any convincing proof.

Other commentators such as Morris (p. 314), Campbell (pp. 164-65), and Rudolph (p. 71) all see Naomi taking Obed to her heart and loving him as if he were her own. The rendering of *ḥeyq* as "breast, bosom" is not only consistent with its usage elsewhere but seems to fit the context here as well. Naomi, in effect, became Obed's "nanny" or "governess."

14. Sasson (p. 172) appropriately draws attention to the fact that these were *šekēnôt*, "neighborhood women," not *našîm*, "women" of the city.

This naming procedure brings up the issue of the child's name, for O. Eissfeldt, *The Old Testament, An Introduction* (1965), pp. 479-80, has pointed out that if *wattiqreʾnāh lô haššekēnôt šēm lēʾmōr*, "and the neighborhood women gave him a name, saying, . . . " is indeed a formula used at name-giving ceremonies, then the actual name should precede the explanation *yullad-bēn lenoʿomî*, "a son has been born to Naomi." He suggests that the name given the child was really *Ben-noʿam*, "son of Naomi," and that this was taken from the text and "Obed" (meaning "servant") inserted. See D. R. Ap-Thomas, "The Book of Ruth," *ET* 79 (1968), pp. 369-73; A. Key, "The Giving of Proper Names in the Old Testament," *JBL* 83 (1964), pp. 55-59; and Gerleman, p. 34. G. A. Cooke, *The Book of Ruth*, p. 18, conjectures that Obed may have been a shortened form of Obadiah. See also Campbell (pp. 166f.), Morris (p. 315), and Sasson (p. 176-78) for a full discussion of this issue.

15. Cox, pp. 143-44.

16. Morris, p. 314.

17. Ibid. See also R. J. Sklba, "The Redeemer of Israel," *CBQ* 34 (1972), pp. 13-17.

18. *The Purpose of Biblical Genealogies* (Cambridge: Cambridge U., 1969), p. 52; see also T. C. Mitchell and A. R. Millard, "Genealogy," *IBD*, 1:546ff. Other children born to Boaz and Ruth would have been counted as theirs. The book of Ruth, however, concentrates solely on the circumstances surrounding the family of Elimelech and "God's steadfast love to the living and the dead" (2:20).

19. KD, 4:493.

20. Ibid.

21. IBD, 1:546.

22. Morris, p. 317.

23. C. H. Spurgeon, *Gospel of the Kingdom* (Grand Rapids: Zondervan, n.d.), pp. 1-2.

24. We should avoid the error made by numerous commentators of presuming that during the writer's time David was king. He became king, but the text of Ruth does not mention him as such. If the book was written by Samuel (as indeed it might have been), then he would have known of David's anointing (1 Sam. 16) but would have died before David ascended the throne.

Scripture Index

Person and Title Index

Moody Press, a ministry of the Moody Bible Institute, is designed for education, evangelization, and edification. If we may assist you in knowing more about Christ and the Christian life, please write us without obligation: Moody Press, c/o MLM, Chicago, Illinois 60610.